WHAT'S WRONG?

Personal Histories of Chronic Pain and Bad Medicine

WHAT'S WRONG?

Personal Histories of Chronic Pain and Bad Medicine

Erin Williams

ABRAMS COMICARTS · NEW YORK

Editors: Samantha Weiner and Jody Mosley
Designer: Pamela Notarantonio
Managing Editor: Marie Oishi
Production Manager: Alison Gervais

Library of Congress Control Number 2023935975

ISBN 978-1-4197-4734-2

Text and illustrations © 2024 Erin Williams

Printed and bound in China
10 9 8 7 6 5 4 3 2 1

Abrams ComicArts books are available at special discounts when
purchased in quantity for premiums and promotions as well as
fundraising or educational use. Special editions can also be created to
specification. For details, contact specialsales@abramsbooks.com or
the address below.

Abrams ComicArts® is a registered trademark of Harry N. Abrams, Inc.

ABRAMS The Art of Books
195 Broadway, New York, NY 10007
abramsbooks.com

CONTENTS

For Dee, Alex, Rain, and Adriana

For Natalie Vavricka
(April 13, 1980–March 4, 2021)

For everyone in pain

"[T]he body is not a thing, it is a situation: it is our grasp on the world and the outline for our projects."

—Simone de Beauvoir

"If you are silent about your pain, they'll kill you and say you enjoyed it."

—Zora Neale Hurston

"Can you not tell that I am militating against sullen acquiescence
Don't you know
That I am fighting to bring on the collapse of
Quiet   well-bred   justice"

—Chase Berggrun

What's Wrong with Me?
Part I

When I was fifteen, I went to my first high school party. I filled
an empty Poland Spring bottle with my mom's sambuca and got
a ride to Jessica's house. I guzzled the caustic licorice syrup and
transformed. No longer the weird, bookish kid with blue hair
and one friend, I made out with a lacrosse player/weed dealer on
Jessica's basement couch. Alcohol, I learned, was the elixir that
alchemized awkwardness into social capital, into power.

Seven years later I sat in the back of an East Village Irish pub,
my regular spot. It smelled like Guinness and piss and one of
the regular's hot takeout food. I'd been "dating" Zach for a few
months, or whenever he wasn't on tour. Zach was a rail-thin singer/
guitarist/junkie without a cell phone. He'd call me exactly every
other night, usually after he was already fucked up, occasionally
after having just left a strip club, and we'd drink more and then
have bad sex in my shitty apartment. On this particular night, Zach
was eating a bag of chips. There was an old hound dog in the bar,
and for several minutes he let the dog lick the neon orange Doritos
cheese off his bony fingers, until they were slick with drool. The
next morning he said, "I didn't wash my hands last night before
putting them inside you." He wanted me to know. I kept sleeping
with him for months. I drank for another eight years.

One of the last nights I had a drink, I had two: well whiskey and Diet Coke in round glasses, a geometric crush of ice, the wilt of condensation. I usually had ten. Before the second drink clunked the bar top, empty before the ice could melt, my body refused to stand. My two dumb legs, wiggly as overcooked spaghetti, collapsed under the weight of me. A friend helped me up, shoved me toward the bus stop. I sat on the little blue bench and vomited uncontrollably onto the sidewalk. It lasted hours. It stopped when I was empty, a pitless peach.

My body refused. My stomach and esophagus, inflamed and abused, waved their ragged, putrid flag.

I'd been in pain for years. Every sip of liquor was abrasive, erosive. I ate candy-colored Tums, little tubes of Rolaids, omeprazole, ranitidine. I doubled the acceptable dose.

The drinking was the most painful part, but it made me forget I had a body at all. I drank until the ache was gentle. The next morning, my voice hoarse, I went back to the medicine cabinet, sulking.

What's Wrong with Me?
Part II

I grew up feeling so much smaller than my own skin, like I was coated in a dense bark of attitude and emotion that was too big for me. I was bullied, assaulted, minimized. All the little pinprick injustices felt like drippy, cavernous, world war wounds.

In elementary school I was nicknamed Cross-eyed Bucktooth Beaver because of my wonky eye and oversize front teeth. The closest friend I had, Brenda, came from an obviously dysfunctional family. We'd always start off playing Barbies and end up with our shorts around our ankles. I didn't understand why we'd had to keep stopping our game, why she'd make me touch her, why it smelled so earthy, why we'd have to hide. I didn't like it. It started in first grade. My body was already an inconvenience, the reason I was teased in public. Now it held more secret discomforts I couldn't name.

I grieve, now, for this child version of myself, the one who never fully experienced the joy of running so fast your chest gets tight, floating in cool waves of chlorinated water after someone does a cannonball, laying in the grass until your skin burns. All of these little pleasures felt like my body was trying to kill me. I thought I'd have a heart attack or drown or get eaten alive by red ants. When the movie *My Girl* came out in 1991, I knew it'd be bees. Maybe quicksand.

I was nine or ten when I had my first panic attack. I'd wake up in the middle of the night and swear I wasn't getting any oxygen. I'd shake my mom awake and she'd tell me to go back to sleep. I'd go downstairs and lie on the couch and try to synchronize my breathing with the cat's, like he could teach me how to do it. I'd turn on the TV to distract myself from what felt like dying. I'd watch *Amazing Discoveries* with Mike Levey, concentrate on the properties of the power steamer or food dehydrator to distract myself from my body.

When I was thirteen, my mom took me to a psychiatrist. I don't remember telling her anything about my life, only what the panic attacks felt like. The doctor gave me five or ten tiny pills, little white sprinkles: Ativan. She said to swallow one whenever I forgot how to breathe.

I wasn't addicted to the pills; they scared me—that quick chemical high, my lack of control over how they made me feel. Alcohol, once I discovered it, was my real savior. It calmed me, soothed my nerves, made me feel like I was part of the same world as everybody else. It was a cure for loneliness, for self-doubt. I never met another drug that could transform me into exactly who I wanted to be. Five shots of vodka from my parents' liquor cabinet was the perfect companion to a Saturday afternoon phone call with a boy I liked. It worked for my parents, and it worked for me.

The older I got, the more doctors and specialists there were. Psychiatrists, therapists, a reiki practitioner who told me all my energy was concentrated in my head. I was diagnosed with depression (manic, postpartum, seasonal . . . a buffet of depressions). I had general anxiety disorder, panic disorder, insomnia, and PTSD. I had bipolar II, with its swinging highs and lazy lows. I've been on more psychiatric drugs than I can name. They made me numb, agitated, calm, or suicidal. One drug's side effects would be mitigated by a new drug, whose side effects would be mitigated by another new drug, until I was on seven or eight drugs at once, a walking zombie. I continued to drink on the pills, because I knew the alcohol was the only thing that really worked. Then I quit the prescription drugs, all at once.

How I Came to Believe That Science (But Not Psychiatry) Could Restore Me to Sanity*

*I AM NOT A SCIENTOLOGIST. Keep reading.

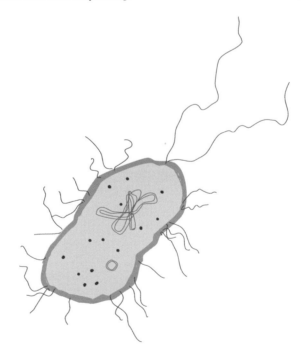

Self-portrait as a
single-celled organism

One of alcohol's mysterious charms is that, if consumed with enough enthusiasm and regularity, it makes you delusional. Deep into my own alcoholic bottom (what people in my sober club call the darkest moments of your addicted life), I decided to leave my steady job as a data analyst in finance and go back to school to study science. In my mind, I was going to become a dietitian, to teach others about healthy living. Never mind my pack-a-day smoking habit or raging substance use disorder. I would invent the next green juice, move to Los Angeles, start wearing a lot of sterling silver rings and help celebrities learn to intuitively eat raw almonds.

A few weeks into my first semester, a few chapters deep into my biology textbook, I braved my first day without alcohol. On a morning like so many others (pounding headache, wide-open front door, black haze where last night's memories should have been), I woke up and knew I needed to stop. It was a choice between life or not life. Like the nano-organisms that saturated my days, I would survive this extreme heat, the volcanic eruption of shame that filled me to the brim.

As I wrung myself out, poured whatever was left in the bottles down the generic, apartment-grade toilet, I filled back up with science. School was my lighthouse, the beam that guided me safely into my new life. I had to learn how to talk to people again, how to tell the difference between romance and exploitation, what safety felt like. I also learned how DNA is cut and how Darwin changed the world.

Newly sober, nothing made sense. I had no plan for living, no routines. Feelings and memories would well up inside me out of nowhere. I would wither at the slightest touch, my body remembering those slobber-coated fingers reaching toward my cervix.

But science: it was clear. Objective. In my strange new reality, where everything felt partial, illusory, and deeply personal, it promised cold, clean facts. A prokaryote could survive the harshest environments. Douse it liberally with antibiotics and it would learn to grow despite human industry. Each element of the architecture of a cell was the stunning consummation of millennia of data.

Science became my guiding light. It was Truth, my Higher Power, the only certainty I could rely on as my entire world caved in. I became a retweeter of chemistry memes. I made Carl Sagan quotes into art prints and cross-stitched Neil deGrasse Tyson's face into a pillow. Loving science became my entire personality.

While in school, I started volunteering at a cancer hospital, taking lunch orders for patients receiving outpatient chemotherapy. I got warm blankets for their legs as their toes began to go numb, the noxious drip of clear chemistry filtering from bag to tube to needle to vein.

For the first few shifts, I took breaks to cry in the bathroom. It was devastating to be in the presence of so many sick people. As I got to know someone—whether they ran hot or cold, preferred ginger ale or apple juice—I would see them materially deteriorate from week to week. It was incredibly uncomfortable work, but passing out menus and delivering brown paper bags filled with food made me feel useful in a new way.

I quit school to work at the cancer hospital full-time in clinical research. I'd comb through patient medical records and input little clumps of life into an ancient database. To calculate the exact date of diagnosis for cancer, you had to read about the worst days of someone's life: when they first saw a doctor for back pain or bleeding gums; when routine blood work turned up too many white blood cells; when their spouse drove them to their first terrifying appointment with an oncologist; when a 22-gauge needle first cracked through their pelvic bone to suck out the marrow; when the pathologist first confirmed the proliferation of cancer; when they first calculated their own life expectancy against the days until their child's wedding or the date their first grandchild is due.

You're doing God's work, one of my former financial colleagues once told me in a LinkedIn DM. Medicine was holy. I was part of the divine army, healing the sick with chemical magic, following orders from its disciples in white coats, stethoscopes around their necks like fat crosses.

Jesus Loves Me, This I Know, for He Gave Me Lexapro

I was four years sober when a baby sounded like a good idea.

Pregnancy was wild. My body had never felt productive before, and for the first time in my life, I felt connected to it. Like I *was* my body. I enjoyed sober sex for the first time in my life.

I suppose my fetus also liked my body, because she refused to exit. Two weeks past my due date, I was induced. Latex-coated fingers reached toward my cervix to deposit a little white string. It would ripen my cervix, the doctor said. I imagined the little disk of cells turning pink and plump in the sun like a peach.

Ripen it did not. They tried new strings, new drips, new drugs. I labored for fifty hours before having an emergency C-section, my middle sliced open like a rare steak, drenching the clogs of the nurses and attending surgeon in a rush of warm amniotic fluid.

I struggled to breastfeed my daughter from the moment she was born. She latched like a rabid raccoon, trying to gnaw my nipple off and retreat with it. I was in the hospital, having just labored for more than two days, having not slept in three. The nurses would take the baby so I could sleep, but kept bringing her back in whenever she was hungry. I begged them to give her a bottle so I could rest for more than thirty uninterrupted minutes, but they refused. Instead, they brought in a lactation consultant, an older woman whose mouth clicked and sucked with hard candy. She repeatedly lifted my vampiric daughter's face on and off my bleeding nipple. Back and forth, up and down. She admitted she couldn't get the latch right. She leaned in close to investigate my defective anatomy and dropped a wet Werther's Original from her mouth onto my breast.

After we went home, I kept trying to make it work. I'd try to nurse her one hour and pump the next. Every latch brought searing pain. She'd suck and I'd sob. After four months, I gave up.

Switching to formula brought me so much physical relief, until the hormonal waves inside me spat and crashed and took me down. At first I felt off. It's just a few bad days, I told myself. Then I woke up one morning to the sound of my daughter's cries on the monitor. I walked into her room and watched her scream. I was paralyzed, unable to pick her up and soothe her. I just stared down, weeping. I imagined myself cradling her in my arms as I jumped off the balcony of our two-story home.

It was an SSRI that saved me, and nothing else.

It was a miracle that made me believe that other miracles were possible too.

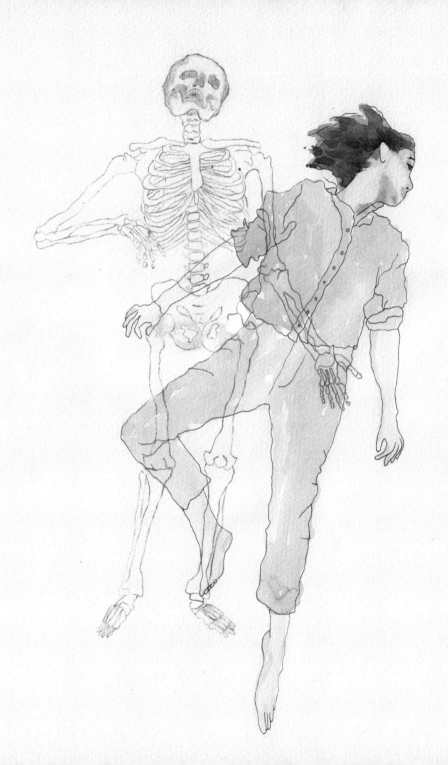

What's Wrong with Me?
Part III

I've had heartburn since I was a teenager, even before I drank. A burning
heart. Psychiatrists don't treat that—you have to see an internist or an
esophageal specialist. I wasn't diagnosed with gastroesophageal reflux
disease (GERD) until I was a few years sober, when the over-the-counter
shit stopped working and I was in near-constant pain.

There was an old man in one of my AA meetings, not actually that old, but
grey-hair old, who had an awful voice, like a toad. Stage IV esophageal
cancer, he told me. I could feel the acid rising in my own throat, could feel
the frogs clawing my larynx with their poison-rich fingers. A few years
away from my last drink, it was time to investigate how much damage had
been done.

I didn't have Barrett's, which is what doctors call the inflamed, damaged
tissue of the esophagus before the cells mutate into cancer and slowly kill
you. I had pre- pre- cancer. Two stops away. To prevent cancer, I would
take twice the normal dose of some acid-taming drug, a minty blue triangle
no bigger than my pinkie nail. I took it for years, at least five, until the
FDA banned it for causing cancer.

Drug Dispenseries: 2050

When the acid was temporarily under control, my body rebelled in other ways. Stomach ulcers. Irritable bowel syndrome. SIBO (small intestinal bacterial overgrowth). I don't have food allergies or gluten problems or H. pylori, the bacteria that causes most ulcers. It's a growing collection of mental disorders paired with various visceral malfunctions, origins unknown. I have a body that attacks itself, or I attack my body. The pain never goes away. It ebbs and flows like a foamy, erosive bay.

Three years into writing this book, another specialist informed me that my GERD was actually NERD, or non-erosive reflux disease. He noted that I was very unlikely to develop esophageal cancer because I am "a thin woman," and it's mostly an "obese male" disease. He pointed at a photo of my esophageal sphincter, an obscene interior shiny pink hole, and remarked how tight it looked. "I don't think you really have high acid," he said. "Your visceral nerves are probably just too *sensitive* to a normal amount of stomach acid."

Too sensitive? And how was I supposed to tell people I'd been diagnosed with NERD?

He's not necessarily wrong. My physical symptoms *could* be my body's response to trauma, stress, and other "mental" problems. In fact, they have to be. The body and mind, what I always thought of as distinct human parts, are intimately connected. Long-term stress, anxiety, and PTSD have profound effects on the body. Scientists agree that the emotional and cognitive centers of the brain communicate bidirectionally with the gut. And my gut, riddled with bad bacterial overgrowth, could clear a room.

But despite all the allergy tests and the endless endoscopies and the antidepressants and the therapy (oh god, so much therapy), I still live without meaningful relief or medical consensus. There are entire days each month that I am in significant pain. I dream about my throat being sliced open and scraped clean.

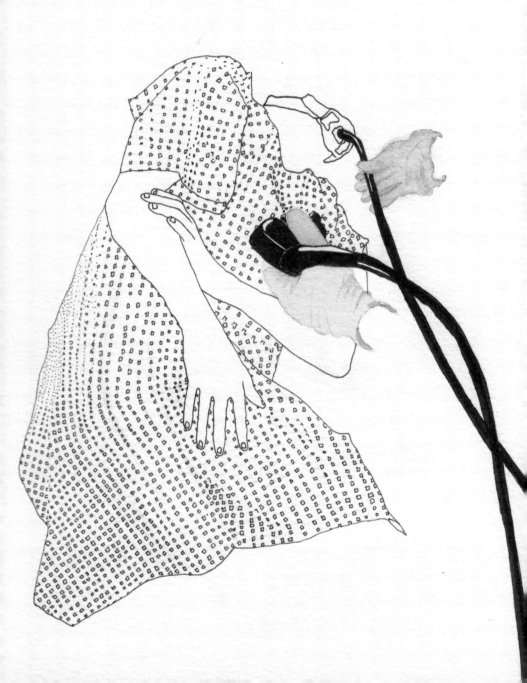

Why do I see one doctor for my mind and one for my body? Why are they treated like two separate things? Why don't specialists across specialties talk to one another? Why did one esophageal specialist see pre- pre- cancer and the other see delicate nerves?

If medicine is science, and science is objective, why can't anyone agree on what's wrong with me?

Medicine can be good at relieving symptoms, treating certain infections, killing cancer, or setting broken bones. Chemically speaking, acid can be tamed by compounds that neutralize it: aluminum hydroxide, magnesium carbonate, magnesium trisilicate. Bases neutralize acids—it's a fact. But then all the bases I ingested stopped neutralizing the acid. At the end of my own understanding of how chemicals and bodies work, at the end of each of my doctors' understanding, I was left without a solution, alone with my burning pain, questioning my reality, scanning search results for a specialist in my area I hadn't already tried.

For anyone unfamiliar, this is what hospital gowns feel and sound like.

According to the CDC, 20 percent of Americans live with chronic pain. That's fifty million people. Fifty million people making doctor's appointments, shuffling from specialist to specialist, filling script after script, often spending their entire lives without meaningful relief. Most of them are people with uteruses.

We know that our health-care system is failing people who live with chronic pain and illness. I know because it's failing me.

I spent the last three years talking to four of the fifty million. This book is a collection of their stories, refracted through my own knowledge and experience.

What's Wrong with Dee?

Dee was born in Brooklyn, but remembers visiting her grandfather in Jamaica as a child.

She remembers the smell of fresh mint, the ripe fruit falling softly from trees, the healing magic of burdock, sea moss, ashwagandha, and sorrel. Her grandfather taught her which fruits to juice, which leaves to pluck, and how to use them as medicine.

"All my aunts passed those things down. We used a lot of those remedies throughout my childhood because [Western] medicine was so expensive."

In one of our conversations, Dee told me how Jamaicans laugh at Americans for having so many trees that don't bear any fruit. In Jamaica, you pick it straight from the tree and eat it. In American grocery stores, the fruit is already dead.

Ackee, the national fruit of Jamaica, is not a native plant. It's thought to have been imported from West Africa in the late eighteenth century on ships carrying enslaved people. Now it drapes the landscape with its yolk-yellow fruit, its giant seeds that bulge out like black balloons when it's ripe enough to eat.

Like most Jamaicans, Dee eats it fried with peppers, onions, and saltfish.

"It reminds me of sitting on my grandpa's lap on the veranda of his house and watching the neighbors mill about."

Dee's mom was a young model who got pregnant after a one-night stand with a man who was in a committed relationship with somebody else. When he learned of her pregnancy, he thought he was the father, but Dee's mother told him he was not. It wouldn't be until Dee was twenty-four years old that a DNA test would confirm paternity.

Dee was born with jaundice and clubbed feet, and was severely underweight at 3 pounds, 5 ounces. "I was always ill as a child. My mother always had me at the doctor's office."

"When I was three or four my mother took me to a psychiatrist because she thought I wasn't talking enough. They shaved part of my head, put nodes on it, and ran some tests. They said I was fine. They said she worried too much."

"The

sky

was

always

falling."

Overwhelmed by the demands of single motherhood while maintaining her modeling career, Dee's mother sent her to live with relatives. Eventually, she ended up in foster care.

"I was in foster care from six to eight years old. My foster parents were from the South, and they had their own healing remedies. I remember going to the garden and learning about seeds and plants. They were strong believers in holistic medicine and healing from the earth. They made everything from plants. I was so happy there."

In the context of widespread health-care disparities, the use of indigenous wisdom about plant medicine is an act of resistance.

In *Working Cures*, Sharla M. Fett describes how enslaved women in America once "asserted their relational definition of health in daily acts aimed at maintaining self and community." Dee learned from her foster family how herbs and weeds and flowers can heal when Western care is inaccessible or unaffordable.

Collard leaves, like the one shown here, were used by enslaved African Americans to treat headaches.

Though her foster parents tried to permanently adopt her after a few years together, Dee's mother fought to retain custody. By then her mother had a new partner. Dee's new caregiver quickly took over the household. He was a domineering, sadistic abuser.

"He controlled everything. I felt like he was giving my mother things to make her weak. She was always sick and throwing up. She developed facial paralysis. He didn't work, but he took her salary and gave her an allowance."

Dee was eight or nine years old when the sexual abuse began. As a result, she started to develop painful urinary tract infections. She never saw a doctor. "They weren't taken care of. I believe they were related to the abuse. No one knew the abuse was happening."

Dee was nine when she began menstruating. Her mother's partner controlled that too.

"He'd give me suppositories to '*manage*' my cycle."

People with uteruses who report having experienced childhood sexual abuse are much more likely to have early onset menarche (periods before age eleven) compared with those who were not abused. Early menarche increases risk for all kinds of health problems, everything from gynecologic disorders to cancer.

As a young teenager, Dee's periods lasted for months at a time. Despite the irregularity, she got pregnant her junior year of high school. After having an abortion in 1994, the school nurse encouraged Dee to get on birth control, specifically an injectable form of birth control called Depo-Provera.

The Depo seemed to make her already-terrible periods worse.

"I kept telling them this is making me bleed so heavily. I couldn't afford good pads or tampons. I had the belt pads. I'd put on two or three of those. I was clotting and bleeding forever. I kept going back to the nurse saying it was making my cycle worse. She told me to *keep going, after six months it will level out.* It never did."

DEPO-PROVERA™
150mg MEDROXYPROGESTERONE ACETATE

Sterile aqueous suspension
1 ml Disposable syringe
FOR INTRAMUSCULAR USE

Though treating heavy menstruation with birth control is common, Depo-Provera is not typically a first-choice option. While white people with uteruses in the 1990s were more likely to be offered a pill, Dee is one of many Black people who were assured by clinicians that temporary sterilization through injection was a better contraceptive option. Injectable or implanted birth control allowed for *clinical* management of reproduction, rather than the *patient* control the pill provides, whether for six months (Depo) or five years (Norplant). To state it plainly: "the pill" was often given to people who were considered socially responsible enough to decide their own reproductive timelines.

As noted by Black scholars and activists Angela Davis and Dorothy Roberts, the sterilization of Black people with uteruses has been considered a solution to socioeconomic problems like crime, poverty, and welfare since at least the 1930s. Failure to suppress the Black birth rate was deemed a threat to the white majority. As Davis wrote about birth control, "What was demanded as a 'right' for the privileged came to be interpreted as a 'duty' for the poor." White folks *deserved* access to reproductive control, but Black people were thought to *require* it.

As Roberts pointedly argues, whatever the terms used are—punitive or incentivized—to pressure Black people not to bear children, "the notion of Black women's control over their own reproduction escapes discussion." Black people's bodies are treated as "objects of social supervision." For example, blaming Black poverty on a high birth rate (Black people having "too many" kids) instead of on the structural systems (mass incarceration, income inequality, housing segregation, etc.) that oppress.

In 1960, Depo-Provera was approved by the FDA for the treatment of endometriosis and miscarriage. It was incidentally discovered that the drug also prevented pregnancy. In the mid-1960s, clinical trials for Depo-Provera as a method of birth control began in seventy-six foreign countries and at one American institution: Grady Memorial Hospital in Atlanta. Grady was severely underfunded and served an almost exclusively low-income Black community. The drug manufacturer's Investigative New Drug (IND) application for Depo was controversial within the FDA because clinical trials had already begun to suggest "an increased risk of breast, endometrial, and cervical cancer."

The average test subject was a poor Black person in their late twenties, unmarried with kids, who hadn't graduated high school. The consent form given to each potential subject was two sentences long and didn't disclose Depo's status as an experimental drug, its contraindications, or its side effects, including that it was "a suspected human carcinogen."

In 1970, Depo's manufacturer was forced to disclose the results of a long-term animal study to the FDA. Some of the animals had developed malignant tumors. Because Depo was the only injectable form of birth control in development at the time, the FDA overruled these concerning animal test results and allowed the human clinical trials to continue at Grady. Physicians could continue to prescribe Depo to people who were "unable" to use other forms of birth control, either because of comorbidities (like cardiac abnormalities) or "mental challenges." (What, exactly, qualified as a "mental challenge" was open to interpretation.)

In 1972, Dr. Michael Popkin, a medical officer working for the FDA, reviewed the clinical studies for Depo, which "revealed four cases of breast cancer, and most significantly, that 'sixteen subjects have developed Grade IV pap smears . . . and subsequently underwent a hysterectomy.'" Another short-term side effect was menstrual bleeding, which occurred in 30 to 100 percent of subjects, depending on dosage. Popkin recommended that, "this IND should be discontinued and no further studies be permitted by the FDA." In the announcement made by the FDA of their decision to ignore these recommendations and keep the IND open with revisions to the consent form, they avoided any mention of cancer or prolonged bleeding.

For the next twenty years, the FDA repeatedly denied the approval of Depo-Provera for general marketing as a method of birth control due to studies that associated its use with cancer, osteoporosis, excessive bleeding, and other side effects. During a Board of Inquiry hearing in 1983, Dr. Sidney Wolfe from the Health Research Group found that one Depo study reported "heavier prolonged bleeding" and another study reported "bleeding so erratic that it amounted to 'menstrual chaos.'"

FDA approval of Depo for general marketing was delayed until 1992, when the World Health Organization (WHO) requested that the FDA eliminate the use of animal studies and accept the use of foreign clinical trial data, even though they "revealed an increased risk of breast cancer and osteoporosis, two risks that . . . continue to haunt the drug's approved contraceptive use" today.

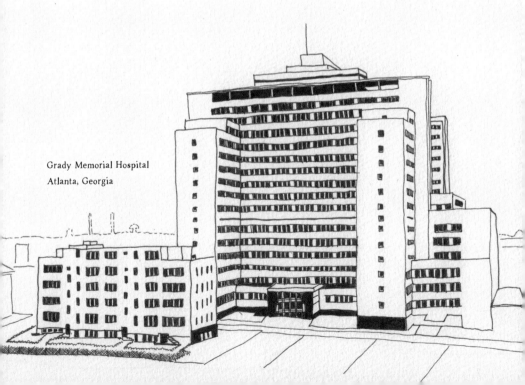

Grady Memorial Hospital
Atlanta, Georgia

Dee wasn't aware of any of this when the school nurse began recommending and issuing injections of Depo shortly after its approval. What the nurse must have, or should have, been aware of, is Depo's contraindication for use with patients who suffer undiagnosed vaginal bleeding.

The nurse told Dee she wasn't supposed to bleed after the first few months, but Dee bled continuously for the first two years.

"I was told to measure the amount. I'd tell them how much blood I lost and they'd say, *That's not possible.* I would pour a menstrual cup out into a container and bring it to the doctor and they'd say, *It'll even out.*"

Instead of taking her off Depo, they started treating the anemia she developed as a side effect of rampant blood loss.

When Dee got to college, she sought another opinion. She told her new doctor she didn't want any more injections. He recommended a vaginal ring and, later, a patch.

After trying several other forms of birth control, including the pill, she went back on Depo a third time. Her doctors assured her that Depo was the only option besides tubal ligation (permanent sterilization). She never missed a shot, was never late for an appointment.

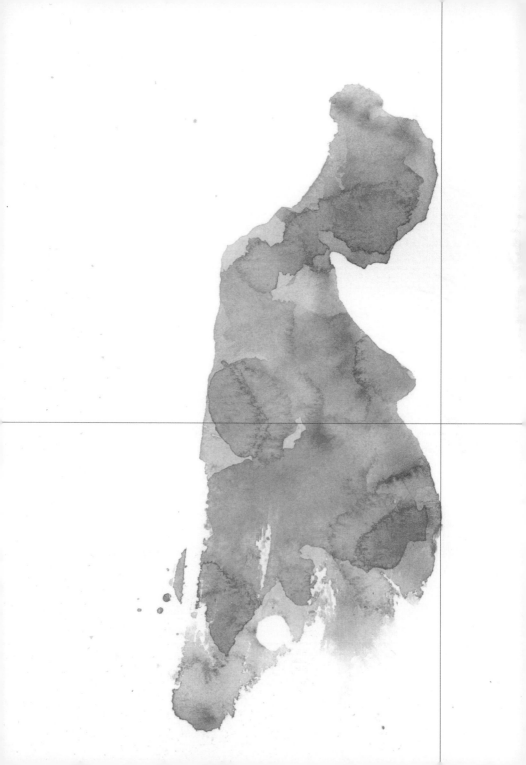

Out to dinner one night, she felt unusually nauseous. She was
in the third continuous month of her period, bleeding every day,
which, for her, was not abnormal. She went to see her doctor
about the nausea. He told her she was three months pregnant. She
asked for an abortion. The doctor told her it was too late.

"I didn't realize I was pregnant because I was still bleeding."

In February 2001, when Dee was twenty-four, her son was born.

She'd met her son's father in 1997. Three years later, she found out she was pregnant.

"I shouldn't have been with him. It was rough. I shoplifted to get food for my son. I'd stopped qualifying for government assistance. I was in that weird space of having massive expenses but not qualifying for help.

"When I finally left him, my son and I bounced around. We stayed with friends. Then I got it together.

"At that point, I was applying for housing. I had an apartment in a seedy place where I was afraid to leave at night. I'd leave early in the morning with my five-year-old son and have to travel without a car. I was an unwed Black mother, and I felt the discrimination then. People thought I was trying to game the system."

Black reproduction has always been plagued with stereotypes of degeneracy, from Ronald Reagan's "welfare queens" to crack babies to the perceived hypersexuality of Black people. These are among other mythologies that deny Black humanity in service of white supremacy.

Dee's bleeding persisted throughout her son's childhood. She refused to go back on Depo. It hadn't done the minimum of what it was supposed to do—prevent pregnancy—let alone tame her menstrual cycle. Her doctors experimented with a range of hormonal birth controls, but Dee felt that her body rejected them after experiencing a continuous barrage of side effects.

"They tried to balance the hormones by using different pills with different levels of hormones. I always felt like it was messing with my skin. I had severe abdominal pain and possible ovarian cysts, stomach ulcers, GERD. Everything was out of whack. My period was either completely gone or I'd bleed for months and months. I switched birth control methods seven or eight times. I felt like I lived at the gynecologist."

The pain grew like a weed.

The pain in Dee's ovaries nearly consumed her. After struggling on various forms of birth control for fifteen years, continuing to bleed, becoming pregnant, and giving birth, Dee had a tubal ligation to prevent future pregnancies. She was thirty-three years old.

"I wanted to get off birth control. The doctor told me the surgery would reduce my cycle. It didn't."

During the procedure, the doctor found large cysts on her ovaries. He assured her that, once the cysts were removed, her abdominal pain would recede. "You should be fine after this," he said.

Dee was still in pain after the surgery. Doctors told her repeatedly that her symptoms were psychosomatic, the result of stress and anxiety. "I think they thought I was a hypochondriac, so I stopped going to the doctor."

"I'm not a big crier. I'm not emotional. My childhood abuser said I always had these crocodile tears. I learned early not to cry. I'd go to doctors and they'd give me a pain scale, and I'd say it's very high, and they'd say I didn't look like I was in pain. I'd research things and say to my doctor, what if I have this? And they'd say I was hysterical. They'd say I wasn't a doctor. They never checked me for the things I asked them to check me for."

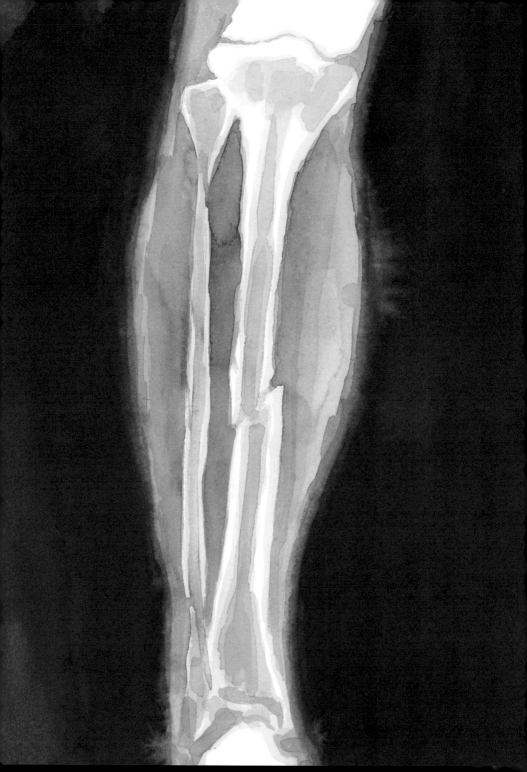

Black Americans are systematically undertreated for pain compared to white Americans. People seeking relief for non-definitive pain in the ER are twice as likely to receive opioids for pain relief if they're white. The reason why Black Americans have largely escaped the hell of the opioid epidemic is because doctors are more inclined to believe in and treat white pain than Black pain, and prescribe accordingly.

The fiction that Black people feel less pain traces its root back to chattel slavery, when white people asserted that Black people could supernaturally sustain corporeal punishment as part of the justification for human enslavement. The prestige of science was used to reinforce the ideology of biological racial differences in order to legitimize the institution of slavery. Physicians were critical players that gave authority to notions of immutable racial differences, whether by describing race-specific diseases or differences in skull size. While we now undoubtedly know that this is bunk science, the effects of these early beliefs are still present in every hospital clinic and affect the experience of every Black American complaining of pain.

Unlike other conditions that can be diagnosed by scan or blood test, pain can't be seen or measured. Doctors, on their quest for objective diagnoses, prefer data collected by more scientific means: microbiology, chemistry, physiology. Pain narratives are tainted by the perceived untrustworthiness of patients, whose true suffering is always obscured by ego and the desire for relief. Physicians may be inclined to think that a patient complaining of leg pain without the corresponding visible fault line in the tibia is at best exaggerating, at worst drug-seeking.

When Dee eventually sought medical expertise again, her doctor offered her a hysterectomy.

Hysterectomies used to be nicknamed "Mississippi appendectomies," because of the frequency with which white doctors practiced them on unconsenting southern Black people with uteruses. More than seven hundred thousand hysterectomies were performed on Black people in the 1970s and '80s alone.

A study published by the National Institutes of Health (NIH) in 2014 demonstrated that Indigenous and Black people in the United States are still significantly more likely to be permanently sterilized than non-Hispanic whites, even though the law no longer openly condones it. As Dorothy Roberts wrote, "the denial of Black reproductive autonomy serves the interests of white supremacy."

Dee explains, "[I later learned that] there was never anything wrong with my uterus. Why did they offer me a hysterectomy? They said it would stop my pain. I complained a lot about the birth control they gave me, and they said I didn't stay on it long enough. They did ultrasounds with a wand, but never the full abdominal ultrasound, MRI, or CT scan like the urologist did later on. None of that ever happened. Maybe if it had, I'd still have a cervix, uterus, fallopian tubes. 'This is going to fix you,' they said. I grabbed onto that."

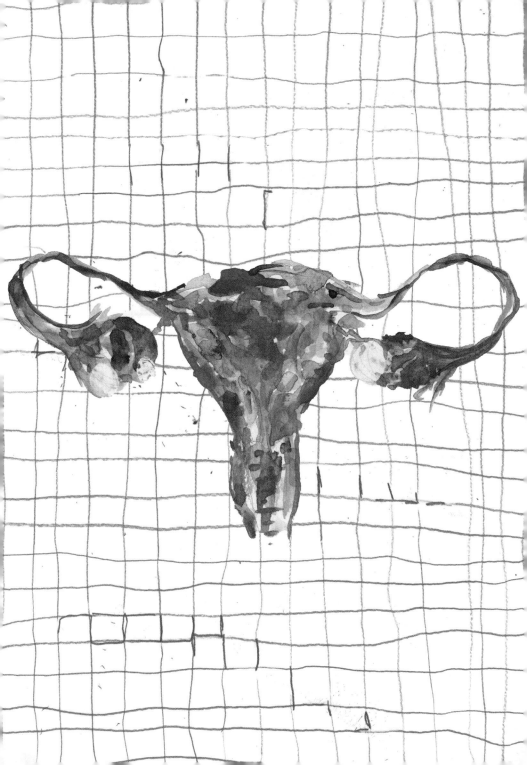

Dee was still in pain months after the surgery.

It's just phantom pain!

the credentialed chorus cried in a common refrain.

It will normalize!

Your body is just healing!

Dee researched the potential causes of pain herself. "I read about granulation scar tissue. Doctors told me there was a small chance of that. They cleared off the granulation and they said there were no issues. They said my body is just getting used to a new state. They said maybe I was doing too much. I stayed home from work for another six weeks."

By the following year, her pain had doubled again. Given some of her symptoms, she wondered if she was having severe urinary tract infections, like the ones she'd suffered as a child. She looked gaunt after losing thirty pounds. She waited months before seeing a doctor, assuming, based on personal experience, that they would not help her.

She had blood in her urine. Doctors initially dismissed her concerns, telling her that the blood was from the hysterectomy healing, but the pain and bleeding continued. When she finally saw a gynecologist, he couldn't tell where the blood was coming from, so he sent her to a urologist.

"The urologist said, 'You have a massive tumor in your bladder. The blood is coming from your bladder.'"

"I gave away my cervix, my uterus, but I didn't have to. All the doctors said the bleeding was normal. I had pelvic and lower back pain. No one ever said, 'Let's run a scan.' When I went to the urologist, he said, 'These are classic symptoms coming from your bladder.' No one checked me for that. They checked me for ovarian cysts, other things, but nothing outside of my reproductive system."

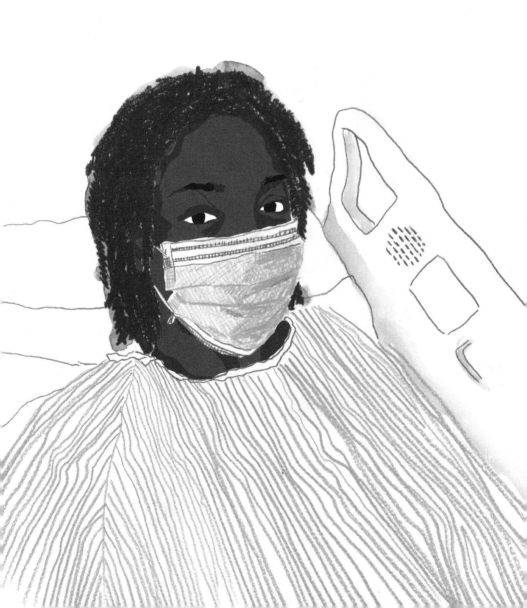

"This is usually a white male disease," Dee remembers her oncologist saying, speaking about the typical demographics for bladder cancer sufferers.

"It felt like he was making an excuse for the delayed diagnosis."

Though white people assigned male at birth (AMAB) are more likely to get bladder cancer, Black people assigned female at birth (AFAB) are more likely to die from it. Research has shown that Black people (regardless of gender assigned at birth) and people with uteruses of any race or ethnicity have significantly higher mortality rates for bladder cancer after controlling for other factors like tumor type and age at diagnosis. According to the American Cancer Society, Black people have the highest mortality rate and shortest survival of any racial or ethnic group for most types of cancers in the United States.

Cancer Death Rates per 100,000 Women* (2014–2018)

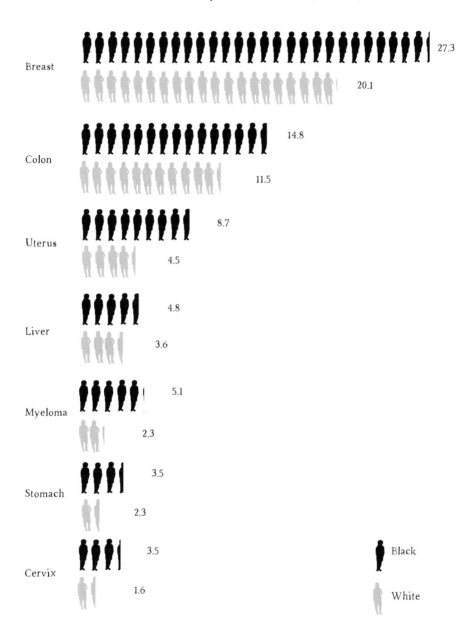

*Language on this page used by the Institute for Chronic Pain.

Source: NCI 2021. Seer Cancer Statistics Review, 1975-2018. Table 1.20

When Dee meets with the doctor for her ongoing treatments, she "feels like an alien, on the outskirts of what I should be. Like I complain too much and the white men don't complain as much. I'm trying to tell him how I feel."

I ask her why she doesn't find another doctor even though I already know the answer. It's the same everywhere she goes. "He's one of the best in his field, so I stay. But I feel completely out of control of my health."

Four days after Dee was diagnosed with stage I bladder cancer, she had her first surgery to remove the tumor, followed by six rounds of chemotherapy. The chemo didn't prevent the cancer from returning, and it left her with a laundry list of other issues. "The urologist told me these secondary illnesses are unrelated to the chemotherapy. He said people always want to blame the chemo. Every time I go to the doctor with pain, they say it's my fibromyalgia."

Fibromyalgia is another pain condition impacting mostly people with uteruses that many doctors don't believe is real. It's a controversial syndrome characterized by musculoskeletal pain, fatigue, and psychiatric or somatic complications. This particular constellation of symptoms has historically been labeled hysteria, nerves, or neurasthenia. Like chronic fatigue, it can be used as a catchall diagnosis for people in pain whose doctors can't or won't find anything else "wrong with." It's most likely to occur in people who have suffered from sexual or other kinds of abuse.

After completing a resection of the tumor and chemotherapy, Dee's bladder cancer returned. She was sitting on the crumpled paper wrapped around the examination table in a clinic when she found out. She started crying.

"It's not the end of the world. I'll give you a chance to compose yourself," her doctor said before leaving the room.

And this is where Dee still is: at "not the end of the world."

"It feels like I'm in purgatory. The doctors told me I'd get my last dose of chemo, but it ended up being a new start to the next phase. I'm constantly walking into the unknown. I'm on a treatment that may or may not work. But the cancer is so likely to come back, I just hurry up and wait. I feel like I'm in *The Matrix* sometimes, like sometimes I can make my own destiny, fix things, make my own future. Shape my own path. At the same time, I have zero control. I have to depend on medicine."

Though she's frequently shuffling between doctor's appointments, Dee—like her ancestors—hasn't entirely turned her agency over to Western medicine.

"My biggest thing is stockpiling healing foods: containers of frozen sea moss, burdock, dragon fruit, cinnamon, whole mint, curcumin. I buy aloe leaves and scrape them, use them on my face and hair and eat some. I juice. I shop at the farmers' market for herbs and spices. I take a lot of supplements."

"I've also been on this path of self-discovery, finding ways to not let cancer be my identifier. I've isolated myself because of the pandemic. I don't feel like a whole person, I feel like pieces. Today if my whole body hurts, I'm just a body. I'm just my reproductive organs, I'm just the particular pieces that matter on that particular day. I'm a mom, a cancer patient, a person who's always in pain."

"I kept thinking I could save myself by hiding my emotions, but actually I have to reach out and build community. *I want to find my joy and be other people's joy.*"

What's Wrong with Rain?

Rain is easily one of the most charismatic people I've ever met. They're a self-described "sad and lonely noise cunt," a ghost masquerading in human skin, a "trans, nonbinary, queer, disabled, and death-positive" little crying witch baby. They make art with contaminated medical ephemera and cast spells in their free time.

Even as a child, Rain felt transitive, incomplete.

"Everywhere I go, people don't see me. I don't register in their field of vision."

Rain has something called X-linked agammaglobulinemia (XLA). XLA is caused by a genetic disorder that prevents B cells from developing normally. B cells are the blood cells that help ward off infections, and without them, you're prone to getting very sick very often.

"It's a rare primary immune deficiency disease. I have no capacity to fight off infection or illness without external medical intervention."

XLA is treatable, but not curable. Once a month since they were three, Rain has gone to the hospital for an infusion of intravenous immune globulin (IVIG). IVIG is a pooled antibody made from plasma extracted from healthy donors.

"Up until then I had all these crazy infections. I kept getting sick all the time. Hand, foot, and mouth; I got the flu a lot; a rash up my entire arm and leg; weird shit. They finally did a full genetic workup on me and my mother, and she was a carrier for XLA."

XLA is an X-linked, recessive genetic disorder. It occurs almost exclusively in people AMAB because, unlike people AFAB, people assigned male only have one X-chromosome. For a queer trans woman, having a condition that seems to contradict who they know themself to be is particularly complex.

"Constantly being told 'you're male,' 'you have a male-centered flaw in your body'— that played into taking me so long to figure out and accept my transition and own my truth.

"My earliest memory is wanting to articulate that I'm a woman. As a young child, I couldn't articulate it. I had no models. I had no language or descriptors. I just knew something was off. I understood that I was different, that I was queer, but I didn't have the vocabulary for it."

Liminality is a concept in anthropology: the disorientation that materializes between two ways of being. People who exist between or beyond the invented binary of gender travel this space. Sufferers of chronic pain and illness also experience this in-betweenness, many of whom consider themselves too well to be called disabled, but too sick for the ordinary rhythms of life. Rain wanders this ghostly purgatory, equipped with effects pedals and post-treatment sharps containers, the materials for their art.

In the book *Crip Theory*, Robert McRuer argues that queerness and disability are linked in their invisibility; both heterosexuality and able-bodiedness "still largely [masquerade] as non-identity, as the natural order of things."

Deviance is defined in contrast to "natural," normative ways of being. Heterosexuality and gender conformity are defined as not being gay or gender-divergent, just as being able-bodied means not being disabled. McRuer argues that compulsory able-bodiedness *produces* disability just as heterosexuality *produces* queerness.

Being able-bodied is defined by your ability to complete whatever physical or mental tasks are required within a system of labor. The categorization of some bodies and minds as heteronormative and others as deviant allows for a hierarchical distribution of resources and power.

Rain grew up in rural Pennsylvania.

"I went to a Christian school. I was in a class with the same eight cisgender kids every year. There was one other disabled student in the school; he had Down syndrome. We were close. My other friends were girls. One would let me wear her clothes. I understood that I was safest around other femme-bodied people. I wanted to do the things the girls were doing.

"I did that stuff in my own home too, but in secret. I'd put on my mom's stockings, bras, and shoes, and do a full face of makeup. I'd hide under the bed if I heard my parents coming. I begged my mom to let me grow my hair out, but she never let me. She'd remind me, *You're not a girl.*"

Rain's relationship with their parents has always been complicated. Their mother worked as a nurse and their father as a pastor.

"For a while, my mom worked with premature babies. I remember being very young and jealous of that. I imagined these babies getting the soft, sweet side of her, and then she'd come home and I'd get the worst—the discomfort and the exhaustion. Now I understand she was coming home to a difficult husband and a sick child and supporting the family. I remember asking:

Once a month, Rain's mom would take them to the Children's Hospital of Pittsburgh for their regular infusions of IVIG.

"I remember that being really laborious for me, both physically and emotionally. But it was also fun. It was a ritual. We'd drive through so many tunnels on our way there, and get lunch together afterward. It was an exciting thing. I remember loving those parts of the trip. Leaving our little neighborhood for the grimy city. Seeing all the old, Gothic architecture, the different kinds of people there. But it centered around this traumatic thing I had to do every month."

When Rain was in fifth grade, their father announced he'd gotten hired by a church in Silver Lake. In 1993, their family moved from rural Pennsylvania to Los Angeles.

"The L.A. riots happened in 1992. It was all over the news. My mom was like, 'You're taking us there?' That definitely speaks to the rural white bubble that we lived in in Pennsylvania. Everyone in our neighborhood was white, cis, hetero . . . We never had anything like that happen. And of course the media sensationalized it. We knew about the riots and that California had earthquakes. That was the impression we had going in. I remember being very nervous but also excited.

"It was a culture shock. L.A. is so diverse. I had so many different people around me. I had visual examples of queer people around me for the first time."

In the 1980s and '90s, the Silver Lake neighborhood was home to a vibrant queer community. Rain remembers a gay bar called Woody's a block from their dad's church.

"It was exciting to me. I remember seeing men in couples going in and out of it. I thought that was really cool. There were one or two gay people at my dad's church too. But it was considered a thing about someone that we all have to live with, not something we celebrate. Like 'this person struggles with homosexuality.'"

Transitioning to a large public school was challenging after the intimacy of Rain's elementary experience.

"I told my teacher and my class that I had XLA. A lot of people made fun of me and didn't want to be my friend. They misunderstood XLA. They'd say I had AIDS. They called me *AIDS boy.* I was just weird! Kids are shitty. They don't understand."

Rain eventually found their community in L.A. They connected with others through music and art.

At eighteen, Rain moved from their parents' house to their partner's house. Rain's mom helped them transition onto Medi-Cal, an insurance program based in California that offers low-cost health coverage for people with limited income. The approval process was difficult, and Rain's coverage was automatically revoked when they turned twenty-one.

"I had preexisting conditions. I couldn't afford my treatments. I became too sick to work. I got sicker and sicker. I couldn't get disability insurance."

Rain had been in a clinical trial at a children's hospital in L.A. Because they'd been participating in a research study testing a new IVIG formula, their treatments were free. Rain filled out patient questionnaires and talked to research associates on the phone about their symptoms. After a few months in the trial, Rain remembers their immunologist coming into the infusion room and saying, "Your meds might be free, but my time is not. The trial doesn't cover my time with you." Rain recalls being told to bring full payment to their next appointment if they wanted to be seen.

"I ended up having a five-year lapse in treatments. Nine months into that I was practically dying of pneumonia. My job had long since fired me. I lost my car. Everyone ran from me. They didn't know how to help me."

Desperate and uninsured, Rain went to a new doctor with four three-ring binders of medical history tucked under their arm to make a plea for a disability evaluation and social security benefits.

"He wouldn't see me for XLA, only for rheumatoid arthritis, which was a qualified disability at the time, whereas XLA was not. The doctor took one look at me and said, 'Give me the short version.' He didn't want to see the files. I wasn't having an RA flare-up that day, so he told me I was lying and threw me out of his office. I walked out of there bawling; I couldn't even talk."

"Doctors say I'm being dramatic. It sucks to be made to feel like my pain's not valid."

What makes pain so susceptible to bias and ripe for political interference is its inherent subjectivity. You can't see pain in someone else, you just have to trust that it's there.

In her seminal book, *The Body in Pain*, scholar Elaine Scarry wrote that:

". . . [often] physicians do not trust (hence, hear) the human voice . . . they in effect perceive the voice of the patient as an 'unreliable narrator' of bodily events, a voice which must be bypassed as quickly as possible so that they can get around and behind it to the physical events themselves. But if the only external sign of the felt-experience of pain (for which there is no alteration in the blood count, no shadow on the X-ray, no pattern on the CAT scan) is the patient's verbal report (however itself inadequate), then to bypass the voice is to bypass the bodily event, to bypass the patient, to bypass the person in pain."*

*Elaine Scarry, *The Body in Pain: the Making and Unmaking of the World* (New York: Oxford, 1985), page 101.

Somewhere within the government's collection of lists, there's a set of qualifying conditions for disability. Denial of benefits to Rain was based on XLA not being categorized as a condition that is worthy of resources. Though Rain also has RA, which *is* considered a qualifying disability, their doctor didn't interpret their pain complaints as bad *enough*.

"When I get sick and it's anything genital related, I wait to see my general practitioner, who doesn't make me feel weird about my body. Sometimes I wait longer than usual because I'm too scared to meet with new or available doctors because so many are super transphobic. There's a total dismissal of my body, even though they're supposed to heal it."

In her book *Tainted Witness,* Leigh Gilmore argues that the association of testimony with the question of whether or not someone is telling the truth, the sorting that authorities must do to divide the pieces of testimony into fact and fiction, "operationalizes a political claim about who gets to decide the question." Marginalized people are still denied the agency and justice afforded to those who have historically been associated with the truth, e.g., the heteronormative, the able-bodied. The pain narratives of patients who don't fall into these categories are subject to shaming and discrediting that other testimony is not. This is an extension of the transfer of power created when the patient in pain, privately an authority of their bodily condition, becomes a source of subjective knowledge to be translated into objective fact by the physician. This power dynamic is extremely problematic for Rain because of physicians' demonstrable bias toward and lack of knowledge about their identity, values, and even anatomy.

"Physicians treat me weird. They don't know what to do with me. They constantly misgender me, even when my chart is right there with an F on it. They invalidate my womanhood. I get exhausted correcting them. I'm generally fairly femme presenting. I'll be wearing a dress and makeup. I'll dress my voice up higher and they still call me 'sir.' They get upset when I correct them."

The medical value of patient pain
narratives declined in the nineteenth
century along with the rise of objectivity
in the sciences, when "feminine"
(subjective) forms of knowledge-sharing
were dismissed in favor of "masculine"
(objective) diagnostic methods. This is
when doctors stopped calling a cough
"a cough" and started calling it "tussis,"
language that alienated patients from a
basic understanding of their own diagnoses.

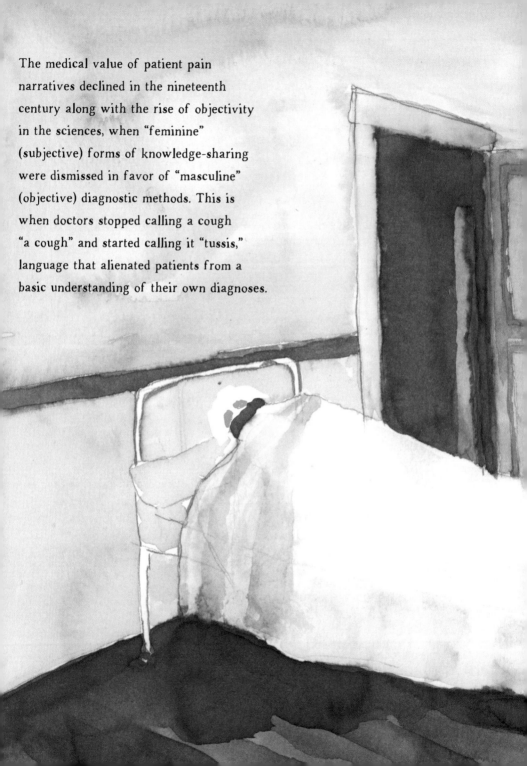

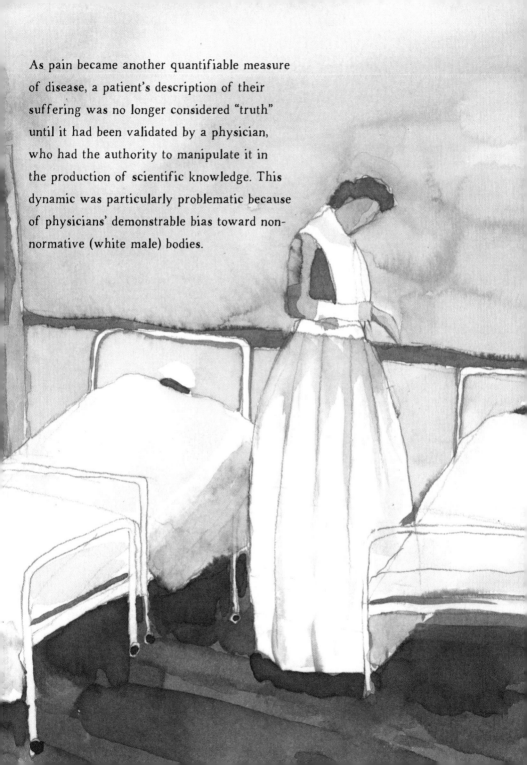

As pain became another quantifiable measure of disease, a patient's description of their suffering was no longer considered "truth" until it had been validated by a physician, who had the authority to manipulate it in the production of scientific knowledge. This dynamic was particularly problematic because of physicians' demonstrable bias toward non-normative (white male) bodies.

Denial of disability benefits had a dramatic effect on Rain's life.

"I had all these medical bills. They went to collections. I maxed out my credit cards filling prescriptions. I was self-medicating on meth. I got into heroin for a period. It was so hopeless and I was in so much pain. I really lost my way."

Rain's father reached out and gave them a choice: move to his house in Nebraska and quit drugs or die in the streets.

"My father and his girlfriend at the time flew out to L.A. and rented a van. We packed up as much of my stuff as we could fit and drove to their house. I detoxed on the long drive over several days. It was awful."

After binge drinking in a dissociative and depressive stupor for the first few months of their Nebraska life, Rain enrolled in school and finished their associate's degree. On a visit to L.A. to see friends, they were introduced to their future spouse. After graduation, Rain moved back to California to be with their new partner.

"After we got married, my wife added me to her health insurance. I was able to afford to go back to an immunologist and resume my IVIG treatment."

Once Rain was healthy enough, they started back at school full-time, first obtaining a bachelor's degree and then a master's in painting and sculpture.

"I realized I might live a frustratingly long time. I thought I should do something with that."

"My work has always been influenced by my sick body. The feeling of detachment. The feeling of being a ghost. The feeling of being trapped in a broken and queer body. I started to make work that would tell my story and provide people a space to consider illness within the context of having a body. Illness exists in many ways, and it's not always visible."

As Rain explains it, "There's an idea in both disability and trans cultures of 'passing.' Passing can mean safety. But it's a bad thing too—it's erasure and assimilation. Invisibility is safety, but at some point, you have to break through that to get to equality and assimilation. I used to want to pass so badly. Yes, I hate getting misgendered every day. But I'd rather be out there getting misgendered being myself. I don't use a mobility device or service dog. People assume that you are healthy, neurotypical. It all comes down to cis-heteronormativity."

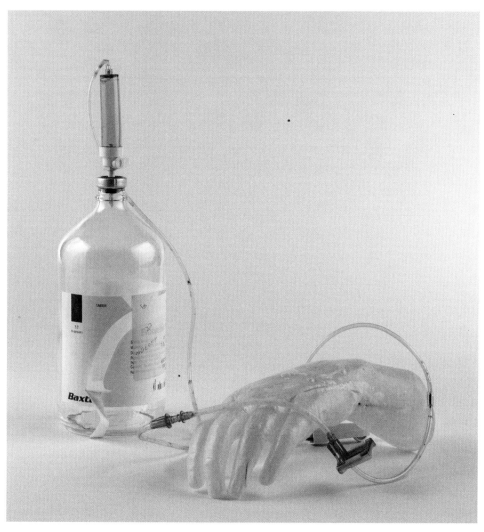

Rain Lucien Matheke
Untitled (Ghost Hand)
Medical Ephemera, Resin
2015

The medical model of disability pathologizes deviant bodies and minds; disability (and queerness) are treated as independent problems. In other words, the disabled person is responsible for adjusting to exclusionary built environments. The medical model sees the person as disabled, not the environment that is disabling, placing no blame and seeking no accountability for socially situated inaccessibility.

The social model of disability argues that variations in ability (whether psychological, physical, sensory, or intellectual) are not inherently disabling; the problem of disability is socially constructed. Systemic barriers, bad attitudes, built environments, and stigmatizing cultural frameworks are what disable people. Instead of demanding that the individual fix themselves (via navigating a health-care system that is demonstrably biased against them), society should accommodate their needs through universal design and inclusive environments.

Both models can fall short in recognizing impairment, like chronic pain, immunodeficiency, and cognitive variances, as disabling. Having a condition that is nationally recognized as disabling can include financial supplementation, though hardly a living wage. According to the Center on Budget and Policy Priorities, the average disabled worker gets around $1,200 a month, and 90 percent of beneficiaries get less than $2,000 a month. If Rain had received disability benefits, it probably would've amounted to around $15,000 per year. California's livable wage is around $57,000.

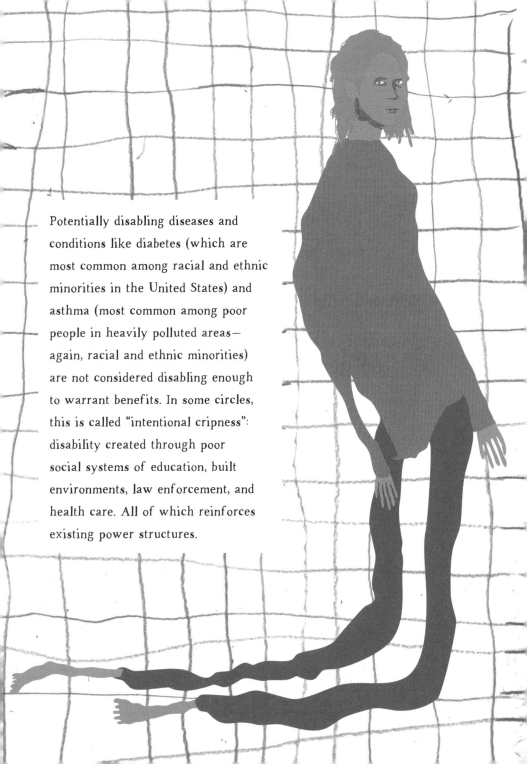

Potentially disabling diseases and
conditions like diabetes (which are
most common among racial and ethnic
minorities in the United States) and
asthma (most common among poor
people in heavily polluted areas—
again, racial and ethnic minorities)
are not considered disabling enough
to warrant benefits. In some circles,
this is called "intentional cripness":
disability created through poor
social systems of education, built
environments, law enforcement, and
health care. All of which reinforces
existing power structures.

Rain doesn't think bureaucrats should get to decide whether they're disabled *enough* to call themself disabled.

"Claiming disability instead of chronic illness is queering it. It's inclusive. There are so many people that fall under the umbrella of disability. I claim disability and come out as disabled because I know I pass as able-bodied on the outside. I'm so tired of everyone assuming that I'm not disabled until I prove otherwise. I want able-bodied people to consider that even if someone looks able, you don't know what their experience is.

"We're taught 'disabled' is a bad word. It's so othering. It shouldn't be. I understand XLA to be an invisible disability. If I overwork my body, my joints swell up like balloons. I get worn out super fast. My lungs are destroyed. If I do anything strenuous, I feel like I'm going to die. A lot of other people with primary immune deficiency would claim to be chronically ill instead of disabled. As I grow, I understand them as one and the same. It is disabling to be sick all the time. My baseline is how most people feel on a day they'd call out sick from work."

For Rain to call themselves queer and disabled is a reclaimation of their power, of the categories that have historically been used to strip them of it. It's a move toward legitimate, subjective embodiment, an assertion of their right to define their conditions with their own language. It's a critique of the normalization of whatever it means to be a person, to inhabit a body.

American transgender scholar and activist Susan Stryker paralleled herself as a trans woman to the monster in Mary Shelley's *Frankenstein* in her work *My Words to Victor Frankenstein Above the Village of Chamounix*. The piece functions as a clapback to those who seek to devalue trans lives based on claims that their bodies are unnatural or fabricated.

Like the monster, Rain struggles to legitimize their subjectivity as someone who exists outside the tightly controlled gendered narrative of acceptable bodies. For Rain, strictly embodying any gender, particularly the one they were assigned at birth, is an "abstract violence," as Stryker calls it. Instead, they move between, above, and around the binary in shadows, permeating the periphery of human possibility, claiming agency where it has historically been denied.

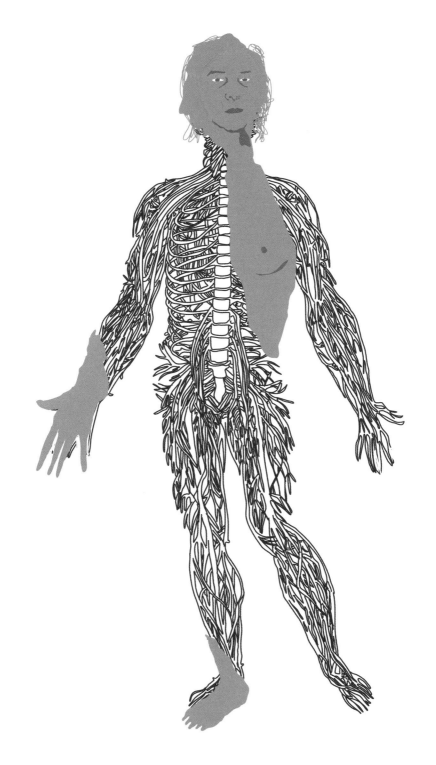

Stryker wrote:

"Like that creature, I assert my worth as a monster in spite of the conditions my monstrosity requires me to face, and redefine a life worth living. I have asked the Miltonic questions Shelley poses in the epigraph of her novel: 'Did I request thee, Maker, from my clay to mould me man? Did I solicit thee from darkness to promote me?' With one voice, her monster and I answer 'no' without debasing ourselves, for we have done the hard work of constituting ourselves on our own terms, against the natural order. Though we forego the privilege of naturalness, we are not deterred, for we ally ourselves instead with the chaos and blankness from which Nature itself spills forth."

As Rain says, "My blood isn't just mine. It's the collective sustaining me."

Rain is referring to the regular infusions of gamma globulin they receive. Each pale bag of medicine hung by their bed, drawn into their arm by gravity, is composed from pools of antibodies from a thousand donors. In this way, Rain's body is quite literally not only their anatomy, but thousands of anatomies—an assemblage of parts.

Rain's alienation is doubled by their illness, which magnifies the complexity of their humanity. The blood that flows through their veins is a medical invention. Each machine filtering plasma is propelled by a jolt of electricity. They are both thousands of people and denied the humanity of being a single person.

"Because I'm disabled, because I'm queer, because I'm openly and visibly transgender, would these people donating plasma even want me to be alive? There's a lot of anti-trans violence in this world. I'm grateful for the compassion that donors have, but I wonder if these people would even want me to live if they knew their plasma was going to sustain a disabled trans woman's life."

"I wonder if, when I get these people's blood energy, I'm getting their essence. Am I taking in their emotions and experiences? Hatred? Bias? Ignorance? Am I literally taking their transphobia into my body?

"I have a fantasy about being able to pin down the thousand people that make up the IVIG dose and be in a space with all of them at once and stand before them and say:

My name's Rain. I'm a queer polyamorous nonbinary trans woman, and I do ritual magic.

"Would they attack me? Execute me? Would they throw me away like trash? Or would they want to see me and feel good about sustaining this life?"

"For a really long time I didn't feel at home in my body. It wasn't right. I was just this brain and spirit trapped in this broken vessel. Since transitioning, that has changed. It's changed even more in recent months. One of my partners, they really see me like I've not felt or seen before. They worship my body and seek to empower my voice. I feel a return to the fluid space I spent most of my life in. I'm no longer running from the ghost of my masculinity, I'm incorporating that back in. I'm allowing my body to be what it is. I'm still taking hormones and growing my breasts. I feel secure, happy, content in this body. As a disabled, non-binary trans woman, I spent so long being so angry that my body was broken, but I've come to accept it, to love it for what it is. I have this understanding, a trust, that my entire system is far more powerful than the dysfunction of my body. I understand that this body is just one part, one component of the integrated whole of myself. That self is, on my best days, a radiant embodiment of love; on my worst days, a frightened crying ghost. They dance together, and I'm learning the steps of that dance. I'm learning the steps."

What's Wrong with Alex?

8:33

◀ Search

ALX

View profile

JAN 8, 2020

Hi, my name is Alex, my friend sent me your post about how you're looking to talk with people managing chronic illness. My doctors have said I have endometriosis. Many of my doctors believe it is what manifested in my body after years of being sexually abused by my doctor. I am one of the survivors of Larry Nassar, the Olympic gymnastics doctor. As I've been through the nightmares and anxiety attacks my whole life, this last year really digging into my past trauma and going to therapy, my body has begun shifting. I still have horrible periods with pain I can't believe sometimes but I haven't been hospitalized for it since I began therapy. And I'm not sure if they are connected but I believe they are.

Message...

Pain and trauma are intimately connected. People with uteruses who report a history of trauma are far more likely to develop several chronic pain conditions, everything from migraines to back pain.

Many studies demonstrate a strong link between pelvic pain and disease and a history of sexual abuse. Some evidence suggests that people who experience abuse suffer greater psychological distress like depression and anxiety, and have worse pain and greater functional disability than those who were not abused.

The Institute for Chronic Pain says that 90 percent of women* with fibromyalgia report trauma at some point in their lives.

And 60 percent of patients with arthritis report a history of trauma.

Upwards of 56 percent of women with chronic pelvic pain report previous sexual abuse.

*Language on this page used by the Institute for Chronic Pain.

Alex was a child gymnast.

"The thing I loved most was the ability to
use every single part of my body and mind
at the same time. It was something I couldn't
experience in any other sport. I could get hurt
if I wasn't really focused and prepared to do it."

Gymnastics wasn't a normal hobby for Alex. She wanted to go to the Olympics. At age seven, she was on a team. By the time she was eleven, she'd more or less dropped out of school, training for eight hours a day instead.

At thirteen, she went to Nationals. She was flinging herself around the uneven bars when her grip doubled under. She flew off the bars, away from the mats, crashing her hip onto the nearby cement. It stung, but she could still walk. She finished her routines and won the competition. Six weeks later, she got out of bed and her leg gave out. She collapsed: her hip was broken. She might have noticed it sooner, had she not been trained to push through pain and keep going.

She began to see her regular team doctor, Larry Nassar, for the injury. He called what he did "treatment." He had been treating her for her other, smaller injuries for two years. After the hip injury, the treatments got worse, Alex said, *because of the area*. He had full access to her pelvis.

"The treatments became much more careless and aggressive and sexual than what was happening before."

Instead of healing her pelvis, he broke it irrevocably. She broke her pelvis off from her head and her heart so she could withstand the treatments. The more she felt, the worse it was. She got hundreds of "treatments."

"I really thought they were medical."

Alex thought the doctor had to align her hip and spine with his fingers inside her.

"Aligning, that was his game. Anything he could align, he would."

Eventually, despite the "treatments," Alex's hip healed. But after all that time healing, without knowing why, Alex wanted to quit the sport she'd loved for so long. Gymnastics was the only thing she'd ever cared about—excelling at the beam and bars had been the guiding principle of her life. She was terrified of quitting, not knowing who she was without the sport. But she couldn't escape the overwhelming feelings of wrongness every time she stretched, bent, flipped, and flew. She didn't have the words to articulate it, but something, she knew, was wrong.

She figured that if she purposefully hurt herself again, she could stop practicing. So she bound down the balance beam in back handsprings one afternoon, threw her hands over the side, and landed on her skull, injuring herself further.

"There was no other way for me to leave."

She told her mom she wanted to quit. Her mom took her to Nassar for more alignment. "The doctor will help you work through this," Alex was told.

Nassar tried to convince her to stay in gymnastics.

"He said, 'If you quit when you're hurt and afraid, you'll regret it for the rest of your life.' That stuck with me. When I'm uncomfortable, I stay too long. I'm afraid of quitting."

Instead of leaving, she got more treatments. She competed for another year.

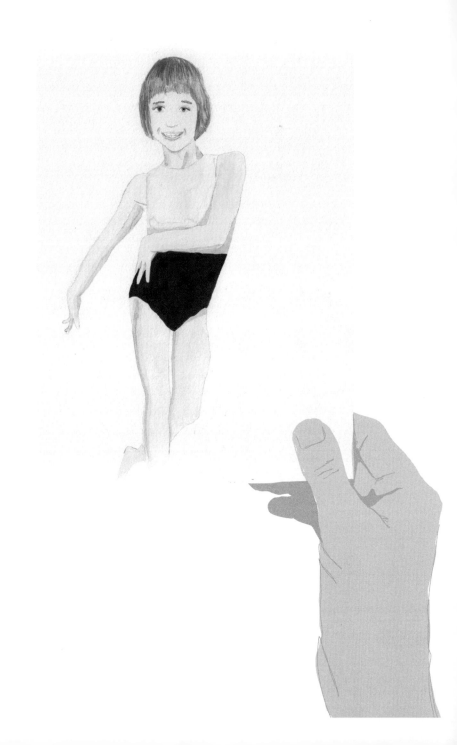

Alex has few childhood memories outside of the gymnasium. She remembers learning to paint Louisiana swamp trees with her grandma, eating her dad's steak and gravy on birthdays and holidays, and riding her bike through the neighborhood with her friend Nick. But almost everything else she did centered around her sport. She was either practicing at the gym, running laps around her house, or stretching in front of the TV while watching videos of competitions. She fell asleep at night in the splits because she thought it'd improve her form. Even while injured, she'd stretch and exercise to stay in shape.

When Alex finally walked away, she erased all the evidence of her life in gymnastics. It felt like everything she knew disappeared.

"I deleted the videos and photos of competitions. I cut everyone out of my life. My only friends had been gymnasts. I wasn't willing to continue to have them in my life, so I had no friends."

"My sister was a senior. I started partying and going out with her. I was angry all the time, just angry and mad at the sport. I ended up making friends, but I didn't have any emotion besides anger."

At a party one night, Alex was drugged, held down, and sexually assaulted. "I don't totally remember that one, but someone stopped it."

She started back at school full-time as a freshman. She was full of pain that she didn't understand—she didn't know why the treatments had felt wrong, didn't fully grasp what she'd survived. "My parents got divorced that year, so I focused my anger on that."

"When I quit gymnastics, I was in high school. My body was so different from the other girls. I was so detached from my body. It wasn't doing the stuff it used to. I didn't like how I looked because of what happened.

"I stopped taking care of my body after the treatments because I felt like it was betraying me. I would eat so much sugar, indulge in these different harmful behaviors to injure my body. I would drink heavily without eating, or not eat all day, or eat so much I'd put myself to sleep. My relationship with food changed. I just didn't like looking at my body.

"The only time I felt like it was worth something was when I was out and when someone would comment on it. It was easy to compliment. That distorted my image of my body. I focused on how to make it appealing to other people and not to myself. I never felt *in* it."

"I still have moments where I don't feel

in

my body."

The kind of dissociation Alex describes may be familiar to other survivors of trauma—it's familiar to me. It's like one's body is a foreign object, a site of betrayal, something to be externalized, mastered, punished, discarded. Dissociation can feel life-saving. As scholar Peg O'Connor wrote, "Often there is a need to make a complete break between subject and object, especially when someone else has so objectified your body that you can no longer understand that body as being part of you." It's a tool for survival that inhibits the body's ability to heal; a cycle of suffering, trauma, memory, endurance. When the body is the site of so much harm, this may feel like the only option.

Anorexia and bulimia are examples of the rejection of the body through starving and purging, evidence of a contentious relationship between body and mind. This idea that they're separate entities, hierarchically arranged, was popularized by seventeenth-century philosopher René Descartes. For Descartes, the mind coerces the body, like a dog, instructing it when and how to fulfill its duties and urges. The body is a hostile, irrational animal to be tamed by the mind in service of the acquisition of knowledge. These characterizations easily conform to heteronormative ideas of gender, seeing the mind as masculine and the body as feminine, where women are considered the presumed subject of male pleasure, and those with uteruses are corporally stuck with the burden of bearing children.

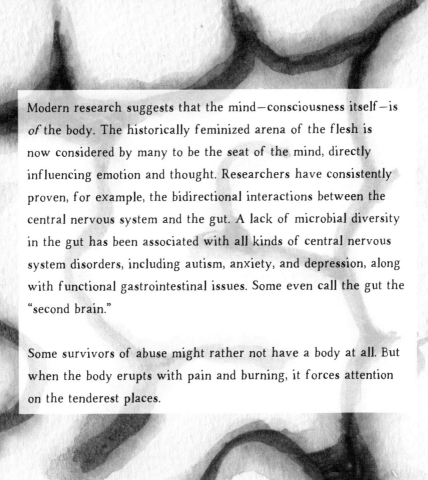

Modern research suggests that the mind—consciousness itself—is *of* the body. The historically feminized arena of the flesh is now considered by many to be the seat of the mind, directly influencing emotion and thought. Researchers have consistently proven, for example, the bidirectional interactions between the central nervous system and the gut. A lack of microbial diversity in the gut has been associated with all kinds of central nervous system disorders, including autism, anxiety, and depression, along with functional gastrointestinal issues. Some even call the gut the "second brain."

Some survivors of abuse might rather not have a body at all. But when the body erupts with pain and burning, it forces attention on the tenderest places.

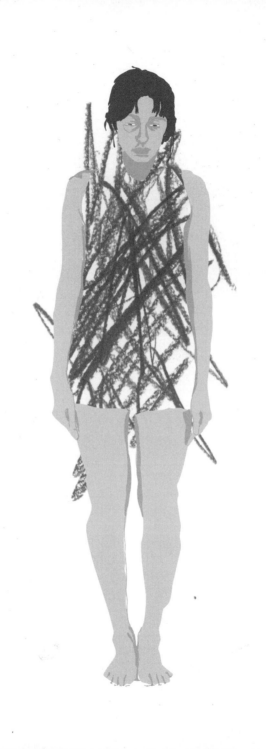

When Alex was a gymnast, she was all muscle, bone, ligament, tissue—all body. Every movement, every bite of food, every minute of rest was in service to how she could bend, how she could soar. When her body became unsafe and she retreated into her mind, she began to punish her body for what it endured. When her body felt good, the way it had when she was a gymnast, it felt, it feels, like a warning of imminent harm. A rush of endorphins, the kind she used to experience after a routine, signals to her body that another "treatment" is near. Her body is trying to tip her off.

"Every time my body feels good, it feels like the other shoe is going to drop. I'm going to feel the emotional pain again. I can't enjoy the fact that I'm able to feel good."

"I had my period once at thirteen, but then it didn't come back. They call it a ghost period."

Up to four-fifths of girls* who participate in intensive athletic training experience this abnormal absence of menstruation due to lack of nutrition and excessive exercise.

At seventeen, Alex got her period for the second time. At first, her periods weren't too bad, but month over month, year over year, they became more painful. She didn't know that the extreme pain was abnormal; she didn't know what having a period was supposed to feel like.

"I wasn't fourteen in women's rooms asking for tampons. I didn't have anyone explaining it. It just seemed like something I was supposed to know. I wasn't in a place where I thought to ask my mom."

*Note that "girls" is the language used by the source study, see notes, page 248.

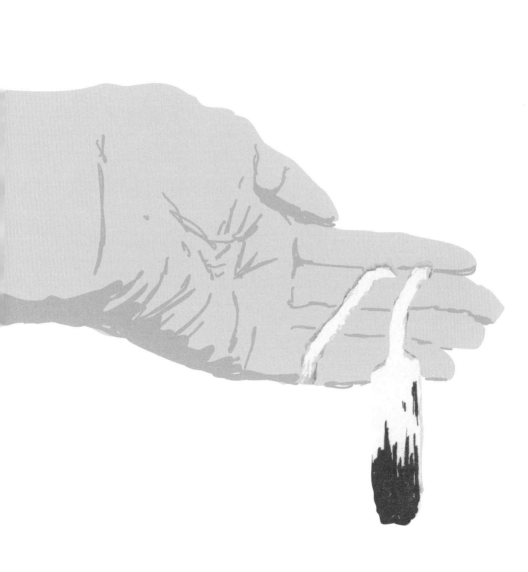

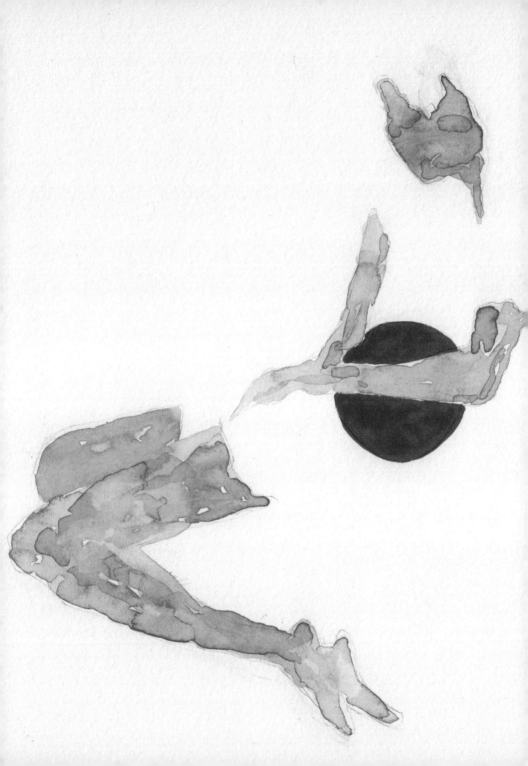

When she was twenty-four, a typical haze of PMS turned into something worse. Alex woke up vomiting uncontrollably. She assumed she'd caught the flu, or maybe the two beers she'd had the night before disagreed with her. She assumed it was her fault. Twelve hours later, she was still throwing up.

"I was so weak, I couldn't lift myself off the bathroom floor."

Her mother carried her to the car and drove to urgent care. Urgent care sent her to the ER due to severe dehydration. When she stopped vomiting, the doctors let her go. They didn't ask about her menstrual cycle or chronic pain.

"I thought that was it."

Alex was hospitalized three more times that year with similar flu-like symptoms. During Alex's fourth hospitalization she got her period, and a nurse made the first connection between the pain, vomiting, and menstruation. She recommended Alex see a gynecologist and consider a workup for endometriosis.

Endometriosis is a painful disorder where endometrial tissue, which lines the uterus, grows outside the womb, attaching itself to other organs and tissue. One in ten Americans with uteruses suffers from it, about six million people, and it costs billions of dollars per year to treat. People with a history of severe, chronic abuse are almost 80 perecent more likely to develop this disorder than those who were not abused.

People with uteruses are more likely to be misdiagnosed in any medical situation, but have particularly poor outcomes and options when it comes to reproductive disorders. This is in part because the uterus and related physiology were originally defined by the medical community as pathological. Because people assigned female at birth have historically been considered essentially as reproducers, "women's health" largely addresses one's ability to procreate. Cisgender men are not exposed to the same kind of reproductive surveillance, including yearly exams of their genitals throughout adulthood. There are few physical positions as vulnerable as having one's feet in stirrups during a gynecological exam. People AFAB have been conditioned to routinely question their experiences of their bodies, particularly their reproductive capacity, and defer to medical expertise (or religious or political leaders) for answers.

Because endometriosis doesn't look or behave one way, and because it's not typically visible on a scan or palpable to the touch, it's often misdiagnosed. On average, it takes ten years to receive a conclusive diagnosis of endometriosis. Its symptoms are diffuse and range from painful periods or bowel movements to excessive bleeding and vomiting.

Insured patients are often shuffled between specialists who craft disparate diagnoses based on the constellation of symptoms they specialize in, from back pain to irritable bowel syndrome. Each specialist assesses and treats a particular issue while patients go years without substantial, integrated relief—without a proper diagnosis.

The deep aching in Alex's pelvis continued to progress, lasting weeks every month. The pain was excruciating.

Even for those lucky enough to have secured a diagnosis of endometriosis, treatment options are limited, and ultimately include surgery to scrape endometrial tissue from areas of the body where it should not be. Alex's doctor recommended birth control or pregnancy as treatment options. She decided against prescribed motherhood, and opted for birth control instead.

Her pain flared in step with Nassar's public unraveling. As Alex's physical condition worsened, charges alleging Nassar's sexual abuse of children were filed in a statement with Michigan police. Her pain crescendoed as more victims came forward.

She tried to ignore the news. A coach at a youth gymnastics team said, "I have known Nassar for years and years. He would never do anything inappropriate." The Michigan Attorney General said at a conference that the two child sex abuse charges against the doctor were the "tip of the iceberg."

Nassar sexually abused more than five hundred children with impunity over the course of more than twenty years. One of the reasons he got away with it for so long is because he treated a very specific type of kid: taught to ignore their screaming bodies, to push through extraordinary discomfort in order to achieve. Alex and her peers were highly disciplined athletes.

Discipline is a form of power that normalizes how people behave and coaxes obedience through careful training, creating what Foucault called "docile subjects." In *Discipline and Punish*, he explains how prisons intend to correct or rehabilitate prisoners: It's the heavily monitored routine that renders them docile. It's the multiple roll calls, the obligatory work shifts, the scheduled meal times—all of it surveilled. Docility is achieved when a prisoner has learned how to manage themselves through adherence to rules they didn't choose, when they no longer require monitoring. This regulated, methodical existence is familiar to any elite athlete. In order to compete, Alex was taught by experts to override her body's signals, taught that freedom was antithetical to success.

Even so, the athletes were never silent. Over the course of at least two decades, many girls reported what was happening with Nassar to their parents, coaches, police, other doctors, administrators, and each other. In each individual instance, the side of the seemingly gentle, effective, if unconventional, expert was chosen over the young girl. "Authority," like the medical authority doctors possess, "is a form of power in which people obey commands not because they have been rationally or emotionally persuaded or because they fear the consequences of disobedience, but simply because they respect the source of the command." It's not just the authority an adult has over a child, but the authority of a medical expert over an athlete, the holder of the key to the kingdom of physical ability that is core to these athletes' identities. Without "Larry," they might have lost their ability to fly.

"I realized everything
from my childhood
had been what I
feared it was."

Alex was abused by the man who was supposed to heal her, to keep her body safe. Now she was sick as a result of the abuse, and she was unable to trust the doctors who might help her, even as her pain worsened.

"I switched doctors a lot. I'd been seeing one since my childhood. I really trusted her. I went a few times as an adult with my pain. My family knew her. It was much different. I'd see other doctors once and I couldn't go back. I'd cry after the doctor and not know why. *Why do I hate this? I hate this.* It started clicking. I didn't know why I didn't trust doctors for a long time either. I didn't know why I was freaking out and crying. When everything came to light, then I realized."

When Nassar's court case began, Alex remained only privately involved. But in March 2018, she went public with her story. The stigma of being a victim of abuse felt overwhelming. But in telling the truth, she started to feel a little bit free. "Going public allowed me to not keep everything so tight and pressed down inside me."

"Not all women are comfortable sharing in public, but they're glad to know they're not alone. I knew a lot of women who'd been raped but didn't know it. Sharing our stories makes it feel less personal, makes it less like we did something to deserve it. We always feel like we're the issue, but now I see it as more of a systemic problem."

Around the time she came forward, Alex began to treat her pain integratively with EMDR, or eye movement desensitization and reprocessing, a type of treatment recommended by Bessel van der Kolk in *The Body Keeps the Score*. EMDR therapy is a research-proven and clinically recognized type of psychotherapy that doesn't require talking through or rehashing past trauma. It helps to resolve the "fight or flight" instinct that occurs when traumatic memories are triggered.

For Alex, it provided some relief. "My head felt less bogged down. I still had a lot of pain during my period, but I could manage it. Before, the anxiety and pain were so twirled together." Her regimen allowed the weeks before and after menstruation to be less miserable.

"It's allowed me to take some emotion out of things. When things start getting really busy, I start to fixate on my body. It becomes that moment where people pick their face or pull out their hair—my obsession is my body or how I look or represent it; I become distorted. I've gotten better at it. This was the first year that I could enjoy just running and feeling good without assuming the rest of the day I would experience something horrible."

She's not used to being okay. She's not cured, but it's becoming more manageable. "I'm not sure if this okayness will stay or not."

She's trying to put the pieces back together. She's trying to feel safe inside a painful body.

"Sometimes I feel really good about who I am and the progress I've made, but sometimes I stare too long or think too hard about what my body has been through, who's used it, and it pulls me back. I feel nauseous; I feel all the usual symptoms. It happens when I'm too happy, when things are going well. All of a sudden, I feel that sense of betrayal again, I want to crawl out of my body. I've had to learn that it can feel good and bad things won't happen."

She learns and forgets, learns and forgets. Unraveling the knots of trauma is the work of a lifetime.

I laughed when Alex told me she watches *Law and Order: SVU* to relax, because I do the same thing. "They do a very good job of not throwing the rape scenes in your face," she said. "Olivia Benson always gets the bad guy, and it's okay. As a survivor, I transport myself into that world. There's always justice, eventually. And the cops all work really hard. It's nothing like you get in real life."

It's so clean, this notion that there's a criminal, and they go to jail and it's over. That the victims just move on once justice is served. It's a beautiful fairy tale for survivors of trauma. The reality is far more cruel: that the seeds of abuse, once planted, take root. That they wrap around wombs and brains and hearts, blossoming into disease. That the systems of power that enable abusers are maintained by the sentencing of a sole bad actor.

What's Wrong with Adriana?

I understand Adriana because she drank like I drank: to disappear. The problem is with reappearing: the bruising headache, the jail cell, the danger to yourself and others.

It wasn't until she was eleven that Adriana realized how heavily her caregiver drank.

"That was when I had to figure out how to feed and clothe two brothers and a sister and get them to school. I never got picked up from swim practice. I would use a pay phone and call the neighbor and have her come. We ate a lot of cereal for dinner. The house was always a mess; there were always dishes in the sink. When my caregiver was sober it was fine, but if they were drinking, it was a mess."

According to the National Institutes of Health, about 15 million Americans over the age of 12 have alcohol use disorder (AUD). Of the people with AUD surveyed, only about 7 percent received any treatment for it the year prior. Excessive alcohol intake accounts for more than 18 percent of ER visits, and about 95,000 people die from alcohol-related causes each year. It's the third-leading cause of preventable death after smoking and poor diet. Excessive drinking is a public health crisis, and most people suffering from AUD don't get the help they need. Eventually, it kills them.

During binge periods, Adriana's caregiver repeatedly drove drunk. The courts got involved and social workers were assigned, forcing them into parenting classes and treatment programs. The help they received didn't result in long-term sobriety.

"For however many hours a week, someone would be in our house observing us, seeing if my caregiver could stay sober. I just remember a social worker always being there. We knew the drinking was a problem. My caregiver was put in the hospital. They were removed from the house. They attempted suicide. Someone would always have to come stay with us. We knew the family services supervision was a signal that home life was unraveling and getting worse. My caregiver couldn't manage their life."

"My relatives would come stay with us—they were the worst people in the world. They rejected the fact that my white mom married an Indian man, my father, and then a Dominican man, my brother and sister's father. They were physically and emotionally abusive."

When Adriana's caregiver tried to commit suicide and was placed in a mental hospital, and again when they were in rehab, another relative would come and stay with Adriana and her siblings. He was a drug addict who gave Adriana weed and different pills to try when she was eleven years old.

In her middle teenage years, Adriana sought refuge from the insanity of living with an active alcoholic in a program called Alateen, designed to help kids understand alcoholism and give them tools to survive it. But at seventeen, in a fog of heartbreak, she picked up alcohol.

Addiction is like that. You swear you'll never be like them until you try it too, and discover how it makes the pain melt away. How it comes to feel like freedom as it closes every door around you.

"By summer of my freshman year in college, my drinking was a huge problem. My Alateen friends told me I needed to go to an alcohol recovery program, so I gave sobriety a shot. It took about three weeks back at college for me to throw that plan out the window."

Throughout her twenties, Adriana continued to battle with alcohol, though she managed to hold down her job and maintain a long-term romantic partnership.

"In 2010, at the age of thirty, I was really struggling with depression for the first time.

"I never knew how to ask for help, and when I had, it never worked out well for me. Getting help didn't feel like a solution for me. My caregiver just drank to forget their problems existed. That's what I learned and that's what I did when I got in trouble."

Adriana had been wary of mental health professionals since her childhood experiences with social services, but she ended up seeing a therapist referred by a friend. The therapist referred her to a psychiatrist, who diagnosed her with major depressive disorder. Adriana went on antidepressants and antianxiety medications. She was prescribed Klonopin and Xanax, highly addictive benzodiazepines, for intense moments of panic.

"Every time I went to see her, she'd end the session with a new prescription.

"I hid that I was drinking from a lot of people. I was running a nonprofit, drinking every night. I kept a plastic sandwich bag of Xanax in my back pocket. I popped a pill every time something was hard. I didn't want to deal with life, so I drank and took a pill. I walked home from work in tears all the time."

Psychiatrists often prescribe highly addictive drugs to addicts because they aren't properly trained in addiction medicine. Many studies proclaim the importance of screening for alcohol abuse in depressive patients and treating it aggressively, but there has been little study of how to treat it. Adriana's psychiatrist and therapist both knew about her drinking, though perhaps not the extent of it. She was prescribed benzodiazepines anyway, and immediately began to abuse them.

While almost 20 percent of patients with psychiatric disorders also suffer from a substance use disorder, psychiatrists spend only a month (2 percent) of their four-year training learning how to treat substance use disorder (SUD). In many psychiatric residencies, addiction training is solely focused on screening, detoxification, and referral, with no instruction on long-term management (though SUD is clearly a chronic, rather than acute, condition). According to a 2021 study published in *Academic Psychiatry*, "This is the largest disparity between illness prevalence and training commitment in psychiatry residency, a disparity which may be influenced by the historical stigmatization of this patient population." Unlike other mental disorders, addiction has historically been viewed as an individual moral failing rather than a chronic illness and public health crisis. Stigma among physicians regarding patients with SUD is associated with "reduced empathy and engagement with patients, reduced delivery of evidence-based treatment services, and poorer patient outcomes."

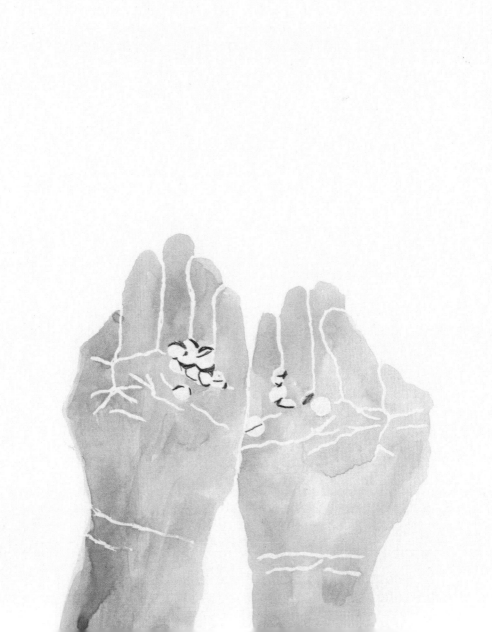

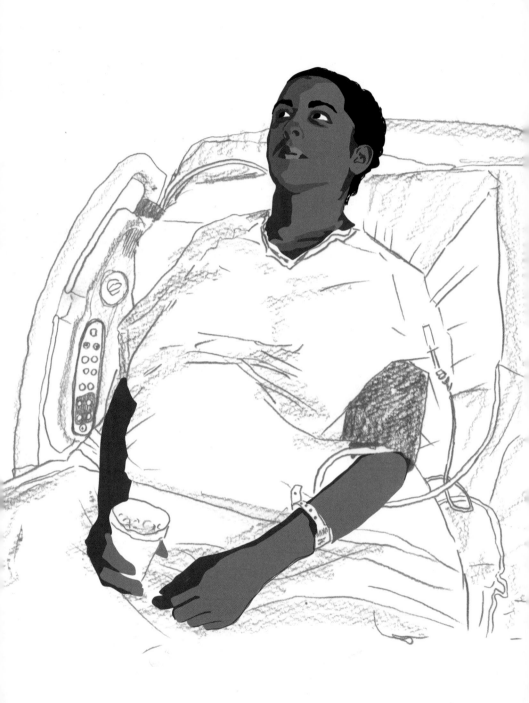

Adriana and her husband thought a move to the suburbs might help, and it did, briefly. She drank less at first, and got off everything besides the antidepressants. Eventually, in preparation for her first pregnancy, she weaned off those too.

"In the summer of 2011, I got pregnant. I quit drinking during the pregnancy. It felt impossible, but I didn't want to take any risks. I felt okay off the antidepressants and alcohol. The change in environment allowed me to be really disciplined, which helped me a lot in a positive way. But I was counting down the days until my baby would be born and I could drink again."

In 2012, Adriana's daughter was born. Her birth experience was traumatic.

"I was in complete shock from the delivery experience."

Though she initially struggled to breastfeed, it soon became a critical part of her relationship with her daughter. Knowing that alcohol would impact her ability to feed her daughter kept her abstinent for a long stretch.

"The second I stopped nursing her, it was a train wreck. I was living in so much anxiety from the moment I woke up until the second I went to bed. I couldn't physically function, I had so much anxiety. I became sad and depressed. That's when I picked up drinking again."

Throughout the first year of her daughter's life, Adriana attended multiple doctors' visits for both herself and the baby. She was never screened for perinatal mood and anxiety disorders (PMADs), despite being so obviously predisposed. She was honest with her providers about her mental health and family history, and that should have been an enormous red flag. Childhood trauma is a predictor of PMADs. Had Adriana been properly diagnosed and treated for her depression and her alcohol abuse, her life may have taken a drastically different course.

Up to 80 percent of postpartum people will experience what some call the "baby blues," the kind of normal instability that comes with having just given birth. Symptoms include crying a lot, not sleeping, and poor memory or concentration. But for one in seven people, these feelings and symptoms can develop into something more serious. They can persist and worsen to include high anxiety, panic attacks, overwhelming sadness, feelings of unworthiness or guilt, and thoughts of suicide or infanticide.

PMADs are the most common obstetric complication today, yet the current standard of care does not include screening. The most available screening tool is a short quiz that postpartum people are asked to complete while waiting for their postnatal doctor's appointment to begin.

These disorders often go undiagnosed despite the availability of such screening tools. Of the people who are diagnosed, only half ever receive any kind of treatment. Studies also show that people of color, like Adriana, experience PMADs at a much higher rate (38 percent) compared with all postpartum people (14 percent). People of color are also more likely to remain undiagnosed even after seeing a health-care provider for multiple postpartum visits.

Postpartum mood and anxiety disorders have been stigmatized since the earliest medical literature. Hippocrates described it as agitation and delirium. In the Middle Ages, people AFAB who succumbed to depression after childbearing were denounced and punished as witches. In the nineteenth century, it was called "puerperal insanity," and accounted for 10 percent of all asylum admissions.

"I was waking myself up with two glasses of wine just to start my day. My husband had no idea I was drinking like that. I wasn't trying to get drunk—just having a couple glasses of wine whenever I needed it, just to get through the pain and anxiety."

Eventually her depression got bad enough that she returned to her previous psychiatrist to restart antidepressants. She was also given a prescription for Klonopin.

"My psychiatrist never mentioned that I could have postpartum depression. I was seeing her once a month, and all she did was check in with me about my meds. I saw a therapist weekly, and my daughter came with me to all my sessions. They never connected the dots between being a new mother and depression.

"I drank to maintain normalcy. I got out of that by getting pregnant again, because it forced me to get my shit together.

"The excitement of having another child and being pregnant helped me get out of that really dangerous cycle. I stayed on the antidepressants, but stopped Klonopin. I stopped drinking. For the first half of the pregnancy, I was in pretty good shape. Then I switched from my previous doctor to a more local doctor at twenty weeks. He told me to stop the antidepressants. He was a medical professional, so I figured he knew. He knew my history, and he still took me off my meds."

The use of antidepressants during pregnancy is controversial. According to *Clinical Obstetrics and Gynecology*, antidepressants are considered by many physicians to be a luxury—rather than essential—medication. Major depressive disorder, like other mental illnesses, many of which are most common in people with uteruses, are seen as different from, and less serious than, other medical illnesses.

Studies show that stopping antidepressants during pregnancy for those with a history of depression causes symptoms to recur in up to 70 percent of people. This has devastating effects on parents, babies, and families. Prenatal depression is associated with increased preterm birth, low birth weight for parent and baby, increased substance use, consequences for infant temperament, and overall worse health status. It's one of the largest risk factors for development of PMADs.

The use of antidepressants and other psychiatric drugs during pregnancy is deeply stigmatized despite a lack of reliable data on how the outcome of stopping them compares with continuation of treatment. Some cite ethical challenges as barriers to this type of research, like randomly assigning pregnant people drugs with unknown effects and a lack of appropriate comparison groups.

In the United States, the health of a fetus is prioritized above the health of the person carrying it, despite data that shows how critical the pregnant person's mental health is to fetal development.

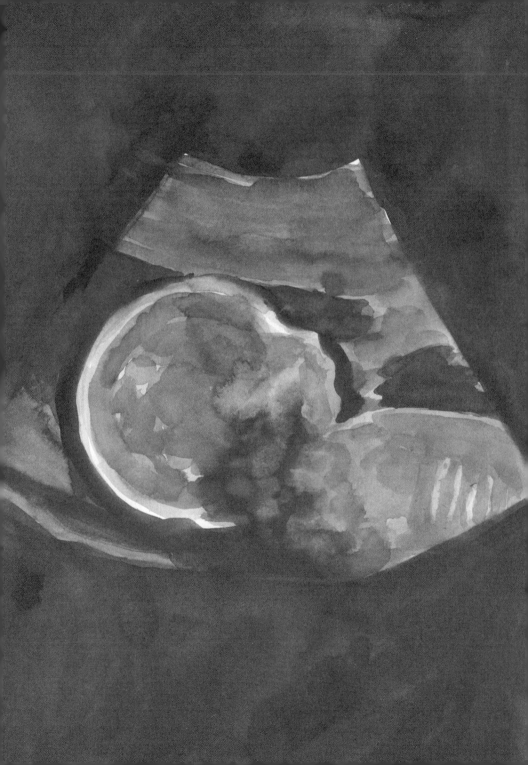

The labor and delivery of Adriana's son was easier than the birth of her daughter had been, but the first few months at home with a newborn and a toddler felt intolerable as she sank deeper into her own sadness. To cope, she began drinking heavily, hiding liquor bottles around the house to keep it concealed from her husband and kids.

Every summer, Adriana's family drove down to the beach for a long weekend with old college friends. Before kids, it had always been a big party.

"It was our first time down with both kids. I was in a lot of trouble with alcohol. I spent the whole trip pumping and dumping and giving my son formula. It was a disaster weekend. I was depressed, drunk, barely doing anything for my kids. My husband was giving them bottles. Then he had to leave early to go back to work. I had to drive back with the kids. My son spent the entire four-hour car ride screaming. I had cases of wine in the house, a full bar of alcohol. As soon as I got back, I ripped open bottles and guzzled booze. I called my husband and said, *I need help. I need to go to the hospital right now.* The neighbors took the kids and my husband drove me to the hospital."

"I thought I was going to kill myself, and the hospital felt safer to me. Someone could take care of me. I remember my room was right next to another mother's, and we were both on suicide watch the entire time. Every wire had to be removed from the room, and the light had to be on constantly. A staff member had to sit outside our rooms the entire time I was there. The door had to stay open."

Adriana was there for two days. For the first time, a psychiatrist diagnosed her with postpartum depression.

"At that point, doctors couldn't stop the train wreck. I was a danger to myself and the kids. I would drink until I was hospitalized. I kept ending up in the hospital. Later, I was admitted to the psych ward for eighteen days."

"A few months after I was released from the psych ward, I took the car to visit family in Connecticut and drove both directions in a blackout. I was driving down I-95 totally drunk, hit the guardrail, and spun out. I pulled into a rest stop and passed out. The cops found me in my car, broke it open, and took me to the hospital. No one knew where I'd been. My husband had called the local police to try and get them to ping my phone. No one could find me. After that I ended up in detox for three days."

Her husband tried to get her into rehab but couldn't find a facility with beds available. They kept Adriana at detox for as long as they could, but then they let her go. Detox is considered an acute care facility, to help clear substances from the body. She was a danger to herself, but physically her alcohol withdrawal symptoms had passed.

"I loved being there. I would've stayed longer. In the detox center, their sole purpose is to assist people physically detoxing from alcohol. I didn't technically qualify based on health screenings. My stats weren't risky enough. I didn't have physical withdrawal symptoms from alcohol. The doctors wanted me to stay longer but they couldn't keep me, with insurance and everything else. I didn't qualify to be there for more than three days."

Leading up to the 2016 holidays, Adriana was in a prolonged period of sobriety and seeing both a psychiatrist and therapist regularly. She'd been doing well for a few months.

"We were going to see family for the holidays. A lot was riding on my ability to stay sober. I did that through the holidays: I stayed sober. I felt relatively stable. It was a huge win to get through that. Things felt like they were getting better, but I was white-knuckling it. I was just surviving. My desire to escape, to drink, to turn everything off, to run away—it was still present and weighing heavily on me."

After the holidays, her husband left for a work trip. Adriana began drinking again as soon as his car pulled out of the driveway. He figured out that she was drinking in his absence, and called her brother and sister to help with the kids. They tried to get her to stop too. It worked for a few days, and then Adriana went back to the liquor store.

"My family left. It was a Friday morning. I'd arranged a playdate for my daughter, who was four. She remembers this. We were supposed to go to Legoland. I promised my kids I'd take them to Legoland. I started drinking that morning. I got in the car. I was so drunk I couldn't remember how to get there. I hit another car that was making a left turn. Both our cars spun out of control. I barely remember the details. I remember screaming that it wasn't my fault. I was terrified. The kids were crying. The cops asked me to get out of the car. They gave me a sobriety test. They arrested me. They took the kids. I sat in the police station with my hands cuffed until they took me to jail. I spent thirty hours in jail, detoxing off of alcohol."

"The entire booking process took so long. They forgot to give me underwear. I was on suicide watch in jail. I didn't have a blanket or a pillow. It was a cold, hard jail cell. I was allowed to leave the cell once a day, and during that time I could have a five-minute shower and one phone call. I couldn't get in touch with anyone. I didn't know if my husband was speaking to me or if I'd ever see my kids again. All I could think about was where I would go get booze if I could get out of that cell. I spent the entire time searching the cell for something I could use to slit my wrists or throat. I was cold and scared. Nobody would talk to me. I couldn't see anything. It was the worst thirty hours of my life."

Adriana's husband posted bail. He drove her to her brother's house since a restraining order was in place, preventing her from seeing or speaking to her children for thirty days. He told her she was going to rehab.

"My husband drove me to rehab the next day. That was the beginning."

Adriana had to pay for the first month of rehab out of pocket, an impossible barrier to this kind of care for most. In order to afford it, Adriana and her husband wiped out their savings accounts and their kids' college funds.

"They checked me in and took my vitals. It had been three days since my last drink, so I wasn't in withdrawal. They dropped me off in a barn space during a women's meeting. There were eighteen women sitting around a table, drinking tea at ten in the morning. I was like, 'Where the fuck am I? Who are these weirdos?' But I was a mess. What do you do with someone like me? I didn't think there was any hope for me. I didn't know if there was a future for me with my family."

"I almost killed my kids. You don't get forgiven for something like that."

While Adriana was in rehab, Family Services began to investigate her based on the charges. They interviewed her friends, family, doctors, and her kids' schools. They compiled a report, which was delivered to her in treatment.

"It was a significant moment for me. Looking at that report, I saw the same accusations that were made against my caregiver when I was a kid: abuse and neglect. I had spent my entire life running away from and hating them, and I did the exact same thing to my kids that they had done to me."

But Adriana found something in rehab that she'd never experienced before: care. "From the minute I was there, I was met with love, compassion, and empathy. People hugged me and said they were so glad I was there. It felt strange, but it felt safe."

Adriana knew that this was her last opportunity to make sense of her life. For the first time, she was treated for both her postpartum depression and her alcohol addiction. Her therapist and recovery sponsor worked together to care for Adriana in a way that had been foreign to her, to help her nurture her bond with her kids, and to produce the court papers she needed to be able to see them again.

"I was facing very serious charges, a class E felony. Because of Leandra's Law, it's a minimum of six months in jail. New York enforces some of the strictest penalties in the country for driving drunk with children in the car. It was in my best interest to stay in rehab as long as possible."

Adriana applied for and received a scholarship to what her rehab called the "extended guest program," allowing her to stay on for an additional three months and serve in a resident advisor capacity, to be of service to other alcoholics seeking treatment. She had to work to maintain that status. It was only offered to two women out of the entire rehab program—those considered to have the highest need.

"I had to demonstrate mentorship and leadership. I was required to go to recovery meetings and share my story, manage the dorm room, and work four shifts a week in the kitchen. By then I loved it: I was so happy there. I made some really good friendships. I was exposed to people who had gone through some really hard shit. So much sexual violence, so much sexual trauma. The rawness, the vulnerability, the community that was built with people who were living on the edge of giving it all up, trying to figure out if they wanted to succumb to their addiction. We were just living in all that, every day, together."

"As I started to heal, I realized I could make a decision. Do I want to go back to my old life? Do I want to be a mother? To try and fix this? Or walk out of here and start over? That reframing was really helpful for me. I didn't feel so trapped in my life. I had the opportunity to look at my life experiences more objectively and from a different perspective."

After four months in rehab, Adriana went home. She avoided jail time, but spent five years on probation.

"I was happy to be with my kids again. I went straight into a recovery program and built some really strong relationships."

"There were three things that I really focused on, maybe four. I had to fall in love with being a mother. I had to learn how to love that. I had to take actionable, intentional steps, commit to a new role and a new identity. I still credit my recovery program for what I learned about addiction. You do the fucking work. It's hard and painful and you're not going to like it. But you have to have faith and listen to what other sober people are telling you to do. You have to be rigorously honest. People loved me, guided me, supported me. And then you have to give what you get. If you want to hold on to what you have, you give it away.

"I'd been in a postpartum group before rehab. I was showing up drunk and wasn't getting anything out of it. When I came out of rehab the woman who'd been running it, who was sober too and knew I was struggling, asked me to run the group. That was a gift. I ran the group in my house. It was the thing I needed the most.

"To create a place for women to come, connect, share, build friendships around really struggling with motherhood. I poured everything into that group. We were meeting in my home, and people brought their kids. The average meeting went for three hours. I hired a neighborhood teenager to watch all the kids upstairs. Some parents couldn't leave their kids, so there were kids who couldn't be in a separate room, kids with behavioral issues. It was a place to show up and be exactly who you were."

Who Adriana is is really quite remarkable. She's a triathlete, a boxer, an executive, an activist, and a really damn good mom. As of the writing of this book, she's six years sober. It's disturbing to think of how close she came to never becoming all of these things, to losing her life entirely.

"Don't be fearful of pain, don't push through it. It's there for a reason. I think if I would've listened to my body earlier, I would've been able to process my trauma earlier. That's an important thing that's been overlooked. We aren't taught to listen to ourselves; we're taught to work through the pain and keep going. We have gut instincts. We're supposed to listen to them. When we stop, we get ourselves into really dangerous mental games. Listen to yourself sooner, even though you're afraid."

What's Wrong with Me?
Part IV

It feels really indulgent to dedicate so many parts to my own wrongness when everyone else only gets one. It's not that my wrongness is *more* wrong than theirs, I just know it better. I can take liberties with my own wrongness that I can't take with other people's. I can make jokes at my own expense. And I know most of my own secrets.

When I was in fifth grade, my class was selected to create the "Kids' News" section of the local newspaper. This was a huge honor, since the paper had every class in every school on the entirety of Long Island to choose from. One special student, I learned, would be chosen at random for the occasion's high honor—a chance to sit down and interview Malcolm-Jamal Warner, who played Theo Huxtable on *The Cosby Show.*

I watched *The Cosby Show* religiously. It was one of the things that modeled normalcy for me as a child, that taught me what being part of a family was supposed to look and feel like. Not only did Cliff and Clair have successful careers, but they were present for their children. *The Cosby Show* was a refuge of corny life lessons, tidy endings, and satisfying resolutions. After spending a day at school getting mercilessly picked on ("Where's the flood?!" my lead torturer, Matt, would inquire about my too-short hand-me-down pants), *The Cosby Show* was my safe retreat. I'm aware of the irony of this now.

Despite not knowing how, I got down on my knees and prayed. *Please God, please, let me meet Theo Huxtable. Please. I will be perfect from now on. I won't lie about doing my homework anymore. Please just give me this one thing, and I'll know You exist. I'll know You love me.*

At ten, I was not a religious person. My mother was an atheist, just like her booming, iconoclastic, severely alcoholic father. Achievement was their religion. My father occasionally said things like, "Jesus was a good guy," but didn't bother with church when he could be nursing a hangover on the golf course.

A week after we learned of the "Kids' News" opportunity, my teacher, Mrs. Jones, made us all sit in a circle around her on the floor while she read off our journalistic assignments. I held my breath. Brian and Melissa would be reporting on chick hatchlings at a local farm. Tabitha would be reviewing a recently published work of middle-grade fiction. Then she uttered my name, Erin, along with the words "jelly bean loaf."

I'd be recipe-testing a jelly bean loaf. A loaf, oven-roasted jelly beans suspended in its crumb.

"Matt," Mrs. Jones spat in her hateful voice, "will be interviewing Malcom-Jamal Warner, star of *The Cosby Show*."

And at that moment I knew: there is no such thing as justice. And there is no God. I never baked the putrid loaf. And I barely passed the fifth grade.

What's Wrong with Evolution?

I told you I loved science, that I thought it saved my life. Newly sober, when everything felt unsteady, I tried to make Science my God. *We have answers!* It promised. *We make everything make sense!* I wanted to feel safe inside a painful body, a body that was beginning to metabolize how desperately I tried to kill it, all the repulsive strangers I'd let inside it. My body burned with secrets, acid, shame.

Survival of the fittest is what Darwin said, but it should be rephrased *survival of the slightly unfit.* Most members of a species are perfectly attuned to their environments, but a few, through random chance, are slightly maladapted. An extra plume of feathers, thickly webbed toes. When the environment inevitably changes, those maladaptations, the things that made them weird, could give them an advantage. They could *become* the fittest.

I took this literally. It became a promise. A psalm.

In church basements I was told by people with more sober days than me that I should find something to pray to.

Darwin and his finches

I emailed my mentor, my high school philosophy teacher
Dr. Sacks, and told him I believed in Science instead of God.

"God is a solution I don't need," I said, as I described the
magic of Amazonian leafcutter ants and the beauty of
human evolution.

Who could possibly require anything more than
the spastic, mosaic beauty that nature displayed so
effortlessly?

2/25/2012

Erin,

You write eloquently about a scientific worldview
here. To "believe in" evolution or any explanatory
framework, however, seems to undermine the
tentativeness and revocability that makes science
so potent a progressive force. Further, science is
concerned with the relationship between large
numbers of things from an external perspective
and has nothing to say about what it is like to
actually be an individual thing. It is more likely art,
rather than science or any bankrupt religious trope,
that demonstrates the contours of an exemplary
subjectivity. Within aesthetic experience you can
see the force of an AA-like submission to a "higher
power." The faith, then, by which to overcome the
tyranny of the present moment is in the form of an
existence lived as a work of art.

What's Wrong with Science?

If Science was my Higher Power, it was a shitty one. *I believe in evolution*, I pined, as recollections of being nonconsensually choked by a college football player flooded my unnumb brain.

A new doctor will figure out why my heart burns, I'd pray, chasing Rolaids with shots of aloe water, which, by the way, is chunky.

Why do we put so much faith in a system that has proven, over and over again, that it doesn't really work?

Voltaire wrote that:

Those who are occupied in the restoration of health to others, by the joint exertion of skill and humanity, are above all the great of the earth. They even partake of divinity, since to preserve and renew is almost as noble as to create.

In the cancer hospital I watched the faithful, cancer
spreading from lung to bone to brain. Faithfully, their
veins were pierced, bags of chemo hung like talismans
above their bowed heads. Their hair dropped in clumps,
their stomach linings shed. They wanted the promise of
another day, another year.

When you spend much of your life in pain, medicine
seems like the only recourse. I made my own pilgrimages
from waiting room to waiting room, begging for relief.

Please just make me comfortable in my own skin, I prayed.
Please help me feel better.

I asked doctors to perform miracles. They gave me potions,
pills, prescriptions. I believed they could heal me.

I believed.

Philosopher John Dewey says that typical notions of "religious experience" should be expanded to include any experience that "effect[s] an adjustment in life, an orientation, that brings with it a sense of security and peace." Function determines value, the old pragmatist instructs.

Lexapro offered me my first religious experience of this sort and, so far, my last.

Once I believed, I kept chasing miracles, kept begging for relief that never came, the landscape littered with false idols.

What's Wrong with Medicine?

When I worked in oncology, the hospital became my church, the site of miracles. Tumor scraped from lung, marrow sucked from bone.

It's been a spectacular fall from grace.

Data was part of its downfall. It promised impartiality, objectivity—and there is no such thing.

Medicine, at its peak objectiveness, becomes science by the careful unraveling and rewinding of context. The gold standard clinical trial is an example of these measures—the blinding and placebo-ing and dice-rolling are all attempts to remove bias from the data, to unearth empirical fact from the messy, context-rich, narrative-laden, chaotic wildness of human bodies.

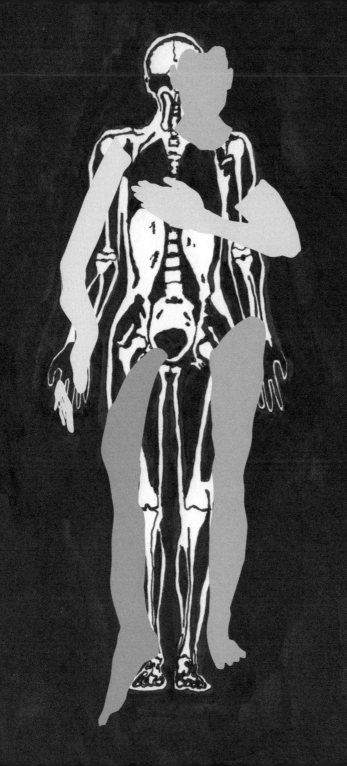

Art has as much to tell us about illness as medicine does.

Pain, like art, isn't fixed, passive, or inert. It's an embodied experience. Like Dr. Sacks wrote in his saucy little email, *Science has nothing to say about what it's like to actually be an individual thing.*

One of medicine's foundational tenets is that only in reducing ourselves to our parts can we become whole. In *Art as Experience*, Dewey wrote, "When artistic objects are separated from both conditions of origin and operation in experience, a wall is built around them that renders almost opaque their general significance . . ." The same is true of rendering human biology an object of medicine. The body as it's lived is layered with social and historical meaning. It cannot be extracted or excused from consciousness. This amounts to nothing less than a denial of humanity.

Disease and illness should be defined as they are embodied and experienced. To call what Dee has "urothelial carcinoma" speaks nothing to what she's endured.* A "good health outcome" for Dee might be defined by her doctors as two cancer-free post-chemo years. But, having read her story, would you actually call any of it "good"?

---

*Most people probably don't even know what urothelial carcinoma is, since nineteenth-century physicians decided suffering should be exclusively understood by people familiar with hoary Latin. Our own conditions are named in languages that are no longer spoken (except for mine—I know what NERD means).

I asked each of the subjects of this book to articulate their suffering again and again and again. Initially it scared me—who was I to ask these strangers for permission to record their darkest moments, their plaguing secrets? Now I understand that the collective work of this project is a path out of solitude. Each of us needed to see each other, and to be seen.

Do you feel seen?

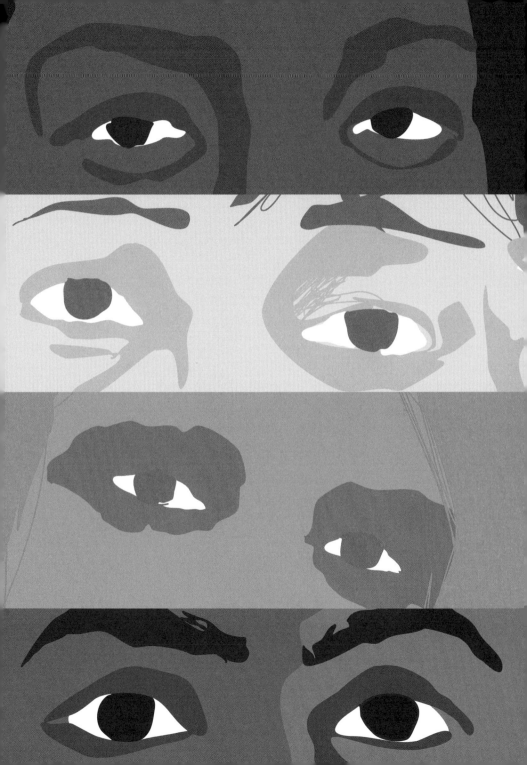

Preserving life must center on care, of which medicine is only one part. Care is holistic, attentive, and focused on the particularities of a person as they are situated in their body, family, community, environment, and world. Care requires safety, vulnerability, and time. It requires that trauma, whether personal, intergenerational, or systemic, is addressed.

In *My Grandmother's Hands*, Resmaa Menakem writes, "We Americans have an opportunity—and an obligation—to recognize the trauma embedded in our bodies; to accept and metabolize the clean pain of healing; and to move through and out of our trauma." I think of Dee's freezer stocked with the herbal remedies of her ancestors, Alex's courage in sharing her story publicly, Rain's sculptures, and the postpartum support group Adriana ran from her home.

It's not solely the private work of individuals to heal from collective harm. We have to recover our stories, share them, trace our histories of pain and suffering across generations, time, and space. We have to hear the stories of others and believe what they say. We have to honor ourselves and everyone else as sites of trouble, grief, suffering, injustice, recovery, and hope.

What's Wrong with Me?

Part V

The summer my daughter was four, I worked fifty hours a week in cancer research and twenty hours writing and illustrating books. When I wasn't working, I was sitting with my dying grandfather as he drank himself to death. I rarely saw my daughter. When I did, she would erupt into violent tantrums, hitting and kicking me whenever I got close.

"GO AWAY, MAMA!" she'd scream, her face flush, her cheeks swollen with tears, her limbs thrusting at me with strength I didn't know she had. Any sweetness I could muster made her wail louder, punch harder.

The tantrums were so disturbing that I resorted to seeing my husband's psychiatrist, a Russian woman with nighttime hours in a dim office on the Upper West Side. In her thick accent, she told me that my daughter's violence was oedipal: she wanted all of her father's love. She wanted to kill me and marry him (again, she was four). She told me that my husband and I should stop holding hands in front of her. She prescribed me gabapentin, an anticonvulsant used to treat nerve pain. It's not a safe drug for addicts like me to take. She called it in, and I never picked it up.

Snuggling my daughter made her fly into a rage. She wanted authority over my body, and I couldn't give it to her. My body reminded me constantly of how it felt to lack control, to be touched when I didn't want it. I'm afraid of physical intimacy on anyone's terms but mine. It felt safer to be absent for myself, for the people who needed my proximity, than to allow my daughter the closeness she needed in order to feel safe.

In winter, she was almost five. Her tantrums were so frequent and murderous that we brought her to a behavioral psychologist, a small blond woman with a white office full of toys. She told me my daughter had "separation anxiety."

When my daughter screamed and hit and scratched and bit, I split. I closed the door to get away from her. I left the apartment and went outside and cried on the street. I resented her for needing me. I thought about my own childhood, and the anguish I felt for a mom who I always perceived as too far away. She, too, worked often and late. Sometimes on a Saturday she'd take me with her to the office, and I'd mess around and create my own pretend businesses, play advertising executive or personal injury attorney. My daughter taps a disconnected keyboard, says, "Mama, I have to do my work."

Work, like drinking, was my escape. I saw another psychiatrist, the one I'd seen for my postpartum depression years before, and told her what picking my daughter up from daycare felt like. Every evening I made the choice between enduring another night as a mother or stepping into traffic to die. She recommended popping a Klonopin before pickup. It's not a safe drug for addicts like me to take. She called it in, and I never picked it up.

For the tantrums to end, I had to give up much of what defined me, the coping mechanisms that had helped me survive. I gave up my research job. I gave up the idea that science could save me. I gave up closing the door on my daughter's tantrums. I gave up running away from her, from myself, from pain.

Inside the worst suffering I had ever known, I started to pray with my whole body, my whole heart. I knew I couldn't get through this alone. I needed the sense of safety and security only a power greater than myself could provide.

In 2012, I told Sacks that God was a solution I didn't need, not knowing that I'd always known God. My first God was alcohol. My second was Science. These gods promised to save me. They never did.

When my guts erupt with pain, when my daughter screams, when I am touched and curl inside myself with fear, I pray. I have a name for God. I call her Susan.*

Susan is a distillation of grandmotherly love. My father's mother, Florence, was one of her highest disciples. She loved unconditionally, cared completely. Being cared for by Florence was having needs met you didn't know you had: a tangle of emerald grapes eaten in bed, a treasure hunt in the old shed where you could keep anything you found, a bowl of velvety mashed potatoes placed beside you at the dinner table.

When I need to feel safe inside the tyranny of the present moment, when my mind or body explode with pain, I ask Susan to help me feel the tenderness of her care. I ask her to help me feel nurtured, loved, and less alone.

Wrapped in the warmth of Susan's arms, I can almost smell the loaves of fresh bread my grandma used to bake. Tangy and sweet. A little musty, because her oven was only a few feet from the cellar door.

---

* "Susan" just seemed like a good grandma-adjacent name at the time.

I had to give my daughter the most
unsettling gift: myself. I had to learn
to be radically uncomfortable, how
to stay when I wanted to run. To
be present for her. To openly hurt.
To collapse and crumble the walls I
spent a lifetime building around me,
the walls that separated me from my
painful body, from the very moment I
am in.

It took years of practice. I'm still
practicing. But now, sometimes, she
curls herself into me, folds into the
vulnerable places and keeps them
warm. I am mothering both of us,
teaching both of us the possibility of a
new kind of ease: surrender.

We all have our own Susans.
We find them in lush gardens,
bursting with fruit and flower;
in rich noise and ghostly
apparitions; in art museums,
churches, mosques, synagogues,
grocery stores, libraries,
orchestras, the water.

We find them in each other.

Notes

Interviews with Dee, Alex, Rain, and Adriana were conducted in person/online/over the phone over the course of several years, from February 2020 through March 2023.

What's Wrong with Me?

According to the CDC: Carla E. Zelaya, James M. Dahlhamer, Jacqueline W. Lucas, and Eric M. Connor, "Chronic Pain and High-Impact Chronic Pain Among U.S. Adults, 2019," Centers for Disease Control and Prevention, NCHS Data Brief, no. 390, November 4, 2020, cdc.gov/nchs/products/databriefs/db390.htm.

What's Wrong with Dee?

maintaining self and community: Sharla M. Fett, *Working Cures: Healing, Health, and Power on Southern Slave Plantations* (Chapel Hill, NC: University of North Carolina Press, 2002), 12.

gynecologic disorders to cancer: Renee Boynton-Jarrett, Rosalind J. Wright, and Frank W. Putnam, "Childhood Abuse and Age at Menarche," *Journal of Adolescent Health* 52, no. 2 (February 1, 2013): pp. 241–247, doi.org/10.1016/j.jadohealth.2012.06.006.

since at least the 1930s: Dorothy E. Roberts, *Killing the Black Body: Race, Reproduction, and the Meaning of Liberty* (New York: Vintage, 1999).

a "duty" for the poor: Angela Davis, "Racism, Birth Control and Reproductive Rights," in *Feminist Postcolonial Theory: A Reader*, eds. Reina Lewis and Sara Mills (Edinburgh: Edinburgh University Press, 2003), 358.

escapes discussion: Roberts, *Killing the Black Body*, 138.

objects of social supervision: Roberts, *Killing the Black Body*, 138.

In 1967: For this section, see William Green, *Contraceptive Risk: The FDA, Depo-Provera, and the Politics of Experimental Medicine* (New York: New York University Press, 2017).

if they're white: Astha Singhal, Yu-Yu Tien, and Renee Y. Hsia, "Racial-Ethnic Disparities in Opioid Prescriptions at Emergency Department Visits for Conditions Commonly Associated with Prescription Drug Abuse," *PLOS ONE* 11, no. 8 (August 2016), doi.org/10.1371/journal.pone.0159224.

1970s and '80s alone: Roberts, *Killing the Black Body*, 90.

non-Hispanic whites: Boynton-Jarrett, et al., "Childhood Abuse and Age at Menarche."

the interests of white supremacy: Roberts, *Killing the Black Body*, 5.

cancers in the United States: American Cancer Society, *Cancer Facts & Figures for African Americans 2019–2021* (Atlanta: American Cancer Society, 2019).

other kinds of abuse: Nia Kaleycheva, Alexis E. Cullen, Robyn Evans, Tirril Harris, Timothy Nicholson, and Trudie Chalder, "The Role of Lifetime Stressors in Adult Fibromyalgia: Systematic Review and Meta-Analysis of Case-Control Studies," *Psychological Medicine* 51, no. 2 (February 2021): 177–193, doi.org/10.1017/S0033291720004547.

an increased risk of breast, endometrial, and cervical cancer: William Green, *Contraceptive Risk*, 16.

a suspected human carcinogen: William Green, *Contraceptive Risk*, 19.

revealed four cases of breast cancer: William Green, *Contraceptive Risk*, 23.

this IND should be discontinued: William Green, *Contraceptive Risk*, 23.

menstrual chaos: William Green, *Contraceptive Risk*, 72.

revealed an increased risk of breast cancer: William Green, *Contraceptive Risk*, 217.

What's Wrong with Rain?

the natural order of things: Robert McRuer, *Crip Theory: Cultural Signs of Queerness and Disability* (New York: New York University Press, 2006), 8.

physicians do not trust: Elaine Scarry, *The Body in Pain* (New York: Oxford University Press, 1987), 6–7.

who gets to decide the question: Leigh Gilmore, *Tainted Witness: Why We Doubt What Women Say About Their Lives* (New York: Columbia University Press, 2018), 15.

their own diagnoses: Mary Fissell, "The Disappearance of the Patients' Narrative and the Invention of Hospital Medicine," in *British Medicine in an Age of Reform*, ed. R. K. French and A. Wear (London: Routledge, 2015), 93–103.

less than $2,000 a month: "Chart Book: Social Security Disability Insurance," Center on Budget and Policy Priorities, updated February 12, 2021, cbpp.org/research/social-security/social-security-disability-insurance-0.

living wage: "Cost of Living Index by State 2022," World Population Review, accessed November 15, 2022, worldpopulationreview.com/state-rankings/cost-of-living-index-by-state.

intentional cripness: Andrew R. Spieldenner, "Considering the Queer Disabled/Debilitated Body: An Introduction of Queer Cripping," *QED: A Journal in GLBTQ Worldmaking* 6, no. 3 (October 1, 2019): 76–80, doi.org/10.14321/qed.6.3.0076.

Stryker, "My Words to Victor Frankenstein above the Village of Chamounix: Performing Transgender Rage," in *States of Rage: On Cultural Emotion and Social Change*, ed. Renée R. Curry and Terry L. Allison (New York: New York University Press, 1996), 211.

What's Wrong with Alex?

Many studies demonstrate a strong link: Andrea L. Nicol, Christine B. Sieberg, Daniel J. Clauw, Afton L. Hassett, Stephanie E. Moser, and Chad M. Brummett, "The Association between a History of Lifetime Traumatic Events and Pain Severity, Physical Function, and Affective Distress in Patients with Chronic Pain," *The Journal of Pain* 17, no. 12 (December 17, 2016): 1334–48, doi.org/10.1016/j.jpain.2016.09.003; C. Liebermann, A. S. Kohl Schwartz, T. Charpidou, et al., "Maltreatment during childhood: a risk factor for the development of endometriosis?" *Human Reproduction* 33, no. 8 (August 2018): 1449–58, doi.org/10.1093/humrep/dey111; Pallavi Latthe, et al., "Factors predisposing women to chronic pelvic pain: systematic review," *BMJ (Clinical research ed.)* 332, no. 7544 (2006): 749–55, doi.org/10.1136/bmj.38748.697465.55.

The institute for Chronic Pain says: Murray J. McAllister, "Trauma," Institute for Chronic Pain, updated August 7, 2017, instituteforchronicpain.org/understanding-chronic-pain/complications/trauma.

Peg O'Connor wrote: Peg O'Connor, "The Cartesian Mind in the Abused Body: Dissociation and the Mind–Body Dualism," in *Dimensions of Pain: Humanities and Social Science Perspectives*, ed. Lisa Folkmarson Käll (London: Routledge, 2017).

functional gastrointestinal issues: Marilia Carabotti, et al., "The gut-brain axis: interactions between enteric microbiota, central and enteric nervous systems," *Annals of Gastroenterology* 28, no. 2 (2015): 203–9, ncbi.nlm.nih.gov/pmc/articles/PMC4367209/.

Up to four-fifths of girls: Cathy Speed, "Exercise and Menstrual Function," *BMJ* 334, no. 7586 (2007): 164–65, doi.org/10.1136/bmj.39043.625498.80.

People with a history: Holly R. Harris, Friedrich Wieser, Allison F. Vitonis, et al., "Early life abuse and risk of endometriosis," *Human Reproduction* 33, no. 9 (September 2018): 1657–1668, doi.org/10.1093/humrep/dey248.

On average: "Endometriosis," Yale Medicine, accessed December 13, 2022, yalemedicine.org/conditions/endometriosis.

Because endometriosis: Jennifer Block, *Everything Below the Waist: Why Health Care Needs a Feminist Revolution* (New York: St. Martin's Press, 2019), 96.

I have known Nassar for years: Kerry Howley, "How Did Larry Nassar Deceive so Many for so Long?" *The Cut*, November 19, 2018, thecut.com/2018/11/how-did-larry-nassar-deceive-so-many-for-so-long.html.

Discipline is a form of power: Michel Foucault, *Discipline and Punish: The Birth of the Prison* (New York: Vintage Books, 1977).

The Body Keeps the Score: Bessel van der Kolk, *The Body Keeps the Score: Mind, Brain, and Body in the Transformation of Trauma* (New York: Penguin Books, 2015).

What's Wrong with Adriana?

According to the NIH: "Alcohol Facts and Statistics," National Institute on Alcohol Abuse and Alcoholism, updated March 2022, www.niaaa.nih.gov/publications/brochures-and-fact-sheets/alcohol-facts-and-statistics.

while almost 20 percent: S. M. DeJong, A. A. Balasanova, A. Frank, et al., "Addiction Teaching and Training in the General Psychiatry Setting," *Academic Psychiatry* 46 (2022): 381–88, doi.org/10.1007/s40596-021-01431-0.

In many psychiatric residencies: John A. Renner, "How to Train Residents to Identify and Treat Dual Diagnosis Patients," *Biological Psychiatry* 56, no. 10 (August 19, 2004): 810–16. doi.org/10.1016/j.biopsych.2004.04.003.

This is the largest disparity: S. M. DeJong, A. A. Balasanova, A. Frank, et al., "Addiction Teaching and Training in the General Psychiatry Setting."

reduced empathy and engagement: S. M. DeJong, A. A. Balasanova, A. Frank, et al., "Addiction Teaching and Training in the General Psychiatry Setting."

Childhood trauma is a predictor: Karmel W. Choi and Kathleen J. Sikkema, "Childhood Maltreatment and Perinatal Mood and Anxiety Disorders: A Systematic Review," *Trauma, Violence & Abuse* 17, no. 5 (2016): 427–53, pubmed.ncbi.nlm.nih.gov/25985988.

Up to 80 percent: Aubre Tompkins, "Postpartum Mood Disorders," *Midwifery Today,* Spring 2017, 38–39.

Studies also show: Jamila Taylor and Christy M. Gamble, "Suffering in Silence," Center for American Progress, October 11, 2022, americanprogress.org/article/suffering-in-silence/.

In the nineteenth century: Nancy Theriot, "Diagnosing Unnatural Motherhood: Nineteenth-Century Physicians and 'Puerperal Insanity,'" *American Studies* 30, no. 2 (1989): 69–88, jstor.org/stable/40642344.

The use of antidepressants during pregnancy: Jennifer L. Payne and Samantha Meltzer-Brody, "Antidepressant use during pregnancy: current controversies and treatment strategies," *Clinical obstetrics and gynecology* 52, no. 3 (2009): 469–82, doi.org/10.1097/GRF.0b013e3181b52e20.

What's Wrong with Science?

Voltaire wrote that: David Woods, "Doctors as Gods," WHYY. PBS, September 4, 2017, whyy.org/articles/essay-doctors-as-gods/.

Philosopher John Dewey says: John Dewey, *A Common Faith* (Clinton, MA: Yale University Press, 1955), 13.

What's Wrong with Medicine?

In *My Grandmother's Hands*: Resmaa Menakem, *My Grandmother's Hands: Racialized Trauma and the Pathway to Mending Our Hearts and Bodies* (Las Vegas: Central Recovery Press, 2017), 37.

Acknowledgments

My biggest thanks are to Dee, Rain, Alex, and Adriana, who shared their stories with me again and again until I got them right. Thank you for agreeing to be part of this work. Thank you for answering my calls, texts, emails, and prayers. And thank you to everyone else who shared their stories with me, bravely and candidly, who aren't featured, but who influenced me greatly.

Thank you, Samantha Weiner, Jody Mosley, Pamela Notarantonio, and the incredible team at Abrams for deftly guiding this book into the world. Thanks also to Paul Lucas at Janklow & Nesbit and Reiko Davis at DeFiore & Company.

Huge thanks to the readers of drafts of this book, who skillfully soothed my anxious brain and provided critical feedback: Kristen Radtke, Kate Novotny, Heather Radtke, Cait Weiss Orcutt, Joy Priest, Chase Berggrun, Kianna Eberle, Forsyth Harmon, Mariah Adcox, Anna Godberson, Elizabeth Crane, and Melissa Febos.

Thank you to Ephemera's Residency at Good Contrivance Farm for providing space for me to work and for believing in this project.

I'm grateful for my friends and family, who have supported me through the many years it took to finish this book. Thanks, Evelyn Orlando and Shannon Frank, for answering all weird medical questions. Thanks, Blythe Adamson, for your support and brilliant scientific mind. Thank you, Mom and Dad. Thank you, Kyle and Lucy. Thank you, Ms. Mary Marlene.

Thank you, Florence Acker Williams, disciple of Susan, baker of bread, grace incarnate. I miss you. I know you would be proud of me.